Th

HOMEMADE GIFTS VINTAGE STYLE

Sarah Moore is a self-confessed vintage-addict and mother of three. She makes and sells vintage inspired pieces at local fetes, fairs and Christmas markets. She is the co-author of *Biscuiteers Book of Iced Biscuits* published in 2010.

HOMEMADE
GIFTS
VINTAGE
STYLE

Sarah Moore

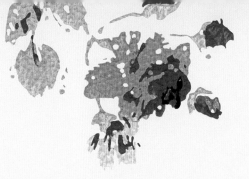

HEARTFELT THANKS TO:

Victoria Sawdon from the brilliant Big Fish design agency for her amazing design, super style sense and gently guiding light through the chintz and vintage chaos.

Debi Treloar – darling photographer who handed out therapy, great breakfast, total access to her fab house, amazing skill and non-stop tea in equal measure.

Beautiful Vicky Orchard and team from the cool Kyle Books for taking on *Homemade Gifts*, rounding us up, putting us straight and making every Monday in March a rare pleasure.

Thanks also to Stevie Congdon for lending us his yacht for the shoot; Maxime Jones-Lloyd for Christmas decorations and the Bootie girls for getting up at dawn to source old stuff with me.

Finally, to all my family for the acquisitive genes, vintage inspiration, total support and the liberty to always do a little of what I fancy; Pete for being a total legend; and my little team, thanks for not eating the easter eggs or opening the advent calendar for all those weeks.

First published in Great Britain in 2011 by
Kyle Books Limited
23, Howland Street
London W1T 4AY

general.enquiries@kylebooks.com
www.kylebooks.com

ISBN: 978 1 85626 941 4
A CIP catalogue record for this title
is available from the British Library

Text © Sarah Moore 2011
Design © Kyle Books Limited 2011
Photographs © Debi Treloar 2011

Sarah Moore is hereby identified as the author of this work in accordance with Section 77 of the Copyright, Designs and Patents Act 1988.

Editor: Vicky Orchard
Design: Victoria Sawdon at Big Fish
Photography: Debi Treloar
Copy editor: Kate Haxell
Production: Gemma John

Colour reproduction by Scanhouse in Malaysia
Printed in China by C&C Offset Printing Co., Ltd

contents

vintage gifts & the handmade revival

This little book is the happy consequence of a passion for all things classic, classy and not available on the high street. Having filled up our house with wonderful old-fashioned things, it was a natural progression to want to share my treasures with other people. Making and searching out vintage items for gifts adds that extra personal element to present giving. You can join in the great handmade revival and relish the resurgence of the homemade gift. There is something for everyone, from those seeking an easy frill for a jam jar to a whole year's worth of gifts from thrift.

Now, obviously, there are some people who might not appreciate being given a slightly battered fifty-year-old enamel teapot planted with spring bulbs or a picnic hamper that is older than they are, or even a corsage made from pretty reclaimed fabric. And for those people you can head to the high street for a gift-wrapped, take-it-back-if-you-don't-like-it, brand-new present. But happily, and increasingly, there IS a whole world of people who adore receiving gifts that are lovingly handmade, carefully chosen, unique and personal. And for all of those 'I saw this and thought of you' types, here is a little book full of inspiring ideas, simple projects and helpful hints for making and collecting presents for all sorts of occasions.

The projects contained in these pages are mostly quick to create – perhaps in an evening or over a quiet weekend – and don't necessarily have to be made from re-found, reclaimed or secondhand materials. But, the sometimes lengthy process of tracking down the perfect piece of material to suit your project, and the great green credentials of making good use of something old, only add to the charm and individual nature of the presents.

vintage hunting

There was an age when all of our homes were filled with useful or pretty little things that were made to last. They were often produced in small quantities or hand-finished, made close to home, from good-quality materials and used or played with carefully. Some bits and pieces were handmade and totally unique, taking hours to create or sew, and were passed down through the generations. This, together with a make-do-and-mend philosophy, meant that, often, no two homes looked the same. And because of these qualities there are still some fabulous examples of vintage-alia to be found.

There are so many places to search for vintage materials. Starting close to home is often a good idea. For sewing projects, look with a fresh eye at the contents of your own and your family's wardrobe. Fabric taken from stripy shirts and flowery skirts, holey woollen jumpers or old aprons can make an eclectic collection of pieces suitable for all sorts of projects. Generations of needlewomen have left a legacy of embroidery,

sewing baskets and handmade pieces, so asking older members of the family or friends is very useful, too. Airing cupboards full of old unused linen, scrap bags packed with trimmings and fragments of old clothes, and boxes in attics are great places to look. It can be really satisfying giving a new lease of life to bits and pieces that are no longer wanted or are too worn to be useful in their current state.

Further afield, there is an almost unending list of thrift and charity shops, garage and car boot sales, auction rooms, vintage and antique shops, street markets, festivals, fairs, fetes and flea markets that have a forever-changing stock of pre-owned treasures just waiting to be bought home.

Finally, internet auction sites provide an always-open shop of listings from every era that you can think of. And these can be delivered to your door without you ever having to get up early for a market, rummage through a box or scale a loft ladder.

I totally and utterly love it and I must have it NOW

You might find that you are drawn to a particular era of vintage, and this can be helpful in defining your style of collecting. And because vintage is just essentially all the things of everyday life in a time past, you can specialise in pretty much anything you like. The secondhand nature of all vintage items, and where you might have to go to find them, means that shopping is not always an instant process. If you are thinking about giving a gift that is a collection of items – such as a sewing basket or picnic hamper – or a present that requires a particular fabric, you need to allow a little time and effort to shop. There is no department store that you can order from, and where there are specialist shops that sell old fabrics or vintage items, there will be a constantly changing selection. So if you find something that you totally and utterly love but have no current use for, or something that you know will make the perfect present in a few months' time, you might find yourself having to buy it just then, because the next time you visit, it will probably not be there.

perfect imperfect

SAFETY FIRST

The rules and safety regulations that cover everything that we buy today were not in place when many vintage items were made, so some commonsense, basic DIY and a good deal of washing, scrubbing and cleaning are often needed when you bring your haul back home. Before you buy any old items, it is always a good idea to check them over thoroughly. The chances are that you will not be offered any opportunity to return a faulty item, and that there is little recourse if your fifty-year-old new favourite find falls apart before it reaches home.

WHAT TO AVOID?

Lead paint, outlawed only recently in the UK, should be handled with care. Anything old that is covered in thick, glossy-looking paint might be a problem. If you really love the piece, send it away to a professional to strip it, or carefully paint over it, but do not attempt to sand or strip it yourself. Have a look on the internet for further guidance if you are worried.

UNSTABLE FURNITURE AND PIECES

If you are not great at DIY, or you don't have a friendly carpenter at your beck and call, it is probably easier to only buy old pieces that are still in good repair.

UNSUITABLE CHILDREN'S TOYS

Lead paint aside, you should also check over any gifts intended for children carefully before letting any youngsters loose on them. Look for worn or loose pieces, splinters, pointy nails or anything that might pinch little fingers.

WORN AND THIN FABRICS

Some old fabrics may no longer be strong enough to upcycle. So thoroughly examine any fabric you are about to buy to make sure that it is suitable for the project that you have in mind. If it is reasonably priced it might be worth taking home a piece that has areas of wear or weakness, but more expensive pieces should be in good, usable condition and able to withstand a good washing, a little ironing and the making-up process.

OLD CUSHIONS

Unpick pretty, old cushion covers or unzip them in order to remove old feather pads and replace them with new ones, as hundred-year-old chicken feathers can be full of dust.

ANYTHING TOXIC OR POISONOUS

Old bottles, jars and tins that have lost their labels should always be treated with caution. If you are worried about what might have been stored in your old biscuit tin, plant it up with bulbs rather than pack it with chocolate biscuits before you give it to your aunt.

CAN YOU CLEAN IT?

Pretty much all secondhand stuff, particularly textiles, will benefit from a thorough clean. Take a good look at whatever it is that you are thinking of buying and make sure you are happy with the condition it is in, or know how to bring it back to its former glory, or how to banish the smell of mothballs.

DON'T RUIN A RENOIR

Do make sure that you are not about to upcycle a priceless antique. However, if something is just clearly past its best and obviously no heirloom, cut it up and re-use it with abandon.

reclaiming fabric

Vintage fabric rarely comes by the metre, unused or still on the bolt, so you will probably find that you will need to reclaim it from curtains, clothes or other made-up fabric sources. Searching out and salvaging what you can is the way forward. Lots of the projects in the book only use small pieces of fabric, so vintage items that have holes or tears or marks that cannot be removed can be a great source of reasonably priced fabric. If you are looking for knitted or woven fabrics, try hunting down old jackets and jumpers. Cut them up carefully so you retain the original finished edges for use in some of the projects.

Some old fabrics are not as colour-fast as our modern equivalents, so don't put your work shirts in the wash with old curtains. If you are particularly fastidious you can unpick the stitches of clothes, but my preferred method is to cut alongside all the seams to produce usable, flat pieces of cloth. Use pinking shears to stop fraying if you like.

The natural hoarder in me likes to recycle as much as I can. So silky jacket linings can cover covered hangers (see page 97). Old buttons are popped in a tin for future use. Ruffled frills from old pillowcases and crocheted edges from worn tablecloths are all carefully reclaimed. Lovely morsels of old lace, monograms and name tags of nobody knows who, cuffs and collars, embroidered flowers, snippets of ribbon and even the smallest piece of fabric are all squirreled away.

For bigger projects, old linen, blankets and curtains provide the largest pieces of fabric. Once again: wash them well before handling them and cut out any marks or areas too worn to use. Look on internet auction sites for suitable blankets, as these are used in lots of projects in this book. You will probably find that they are cheaper to buy in summer, when demand is smaller than in winter.

Finally, don't overlook your own and your family's wardrobe cast-offs. Pretty dresses and well-washed shirts, shrunken jumpers or old velvet jackets: today's fashion is tomorrow's vintage and there may be some amazing finds that have only had one careful owner in a wardrobe near you.

basic kit

You don't need to have rooms full of kit and caboodle to make a perfect present, but here is a short list of the tools that we use in the projects. Great scissors that are properly sharp are essential, so if you are struggling to cut through fine fabrics or thick blankets, invest in a bright, shiny new pair, and then hide them.

Staple and glue guns take a bit of getting used to but they both offer a quick fix alternative to spending ages sewing or pinning fabric, trimmings or baubles that are out of sight. Just make sure that you use them carefully and away from any young helpers.

Also, over the page you will find a long list of vintage items that are in the ingredients lists for the projects. You will be surprised by how many of these things turn up, so if your storage space is limited, and turning your dining room into an Aladdin's cave or your back bedroom into your studio is not an option, then you will need to be quite discerning.

TOOLS

scissors

staple gun

tape measure

pinking shears

glue gun

large pieces of
paper for templates
(newspaper is good)

PVA glue

tailor's chalk

instant glue

pencils

paint and pasting
brushes

little pliers

sewing machine

an iron

safety pins

craft knife

BUY

soaps

polyester stuffing

lavender

bath oil and bubbles

hot water bottles

HOARDING

fake fur

huckaback towels

embroidered linen

tapestry pieces

toy boats

cots and doll's beds

buckles

paste jewellery

brooches

bias binding

military badges
and buttons

cushions to recover

egg cups

decanters

soft woollen blankets

linen sheets

old curtains

sewing and threading
cottons

embroidery threads

luggage labels

chandelier pieces

vintage luggage

glass vases and
mini glasses

old cufflinks

tiny trinkets

wallpaper and
wrapping paper

trims and edgings

out-of-date maps

ribbons

doilies and lace

christmas baubles
and decorations

baskets, hampers
and wicker dog beds

sewing accessories

cutlery

hangers and shoe trees

all sorts of old
crockery and cutlery

buttons

beads

old jewellery

cotton

old fabric of every kind

picture frames

techniques

If you go to great lengths to source just the right old fabric or pretty textile you want to be certain you know exactly what you are trying to create before you reach for your scissors or start to sew. So read through right to the end of each project and gather up your materials before you begin. The list on the page 18 sums up most of the tools you might need too.

The projects in this book do not require any complicated techniques to complete and those that do call for any hand sewing can all be attempted by a beginner. The four simple stitches detailed opposite are all that you need in order to make the lovely vintage gifts in the Sewn by Hand chapter.

If you do have a sewing machine then you can use it for some of the hand-sewn projects for a speedier result, but if not then a needle and thread will be more than sufficient.

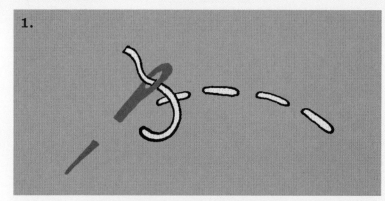

1. RUNNING STITCH

This is the simplest straight-line stitch that you can use. Simply knot the end of your thread and pass your needle in and out through the fabric, leaving behind a trail of even little stitches in the size that you need. For the neatest results, pull your thread completely through each time you stitch, rather than feeding several stitches onto the needle at the same time.

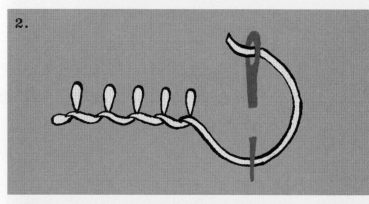

2. BLANKET STITCH

This is a really useful stitch for edging unfinished material or joining two pieces together. Work stitch from left to right. Insert the needle from front to back before you pull the needle through the fabric, carry the thread under the point of the needles as seen in the illustration. Keep repeating this and a little line of thread will appear on the edge of the fabric.

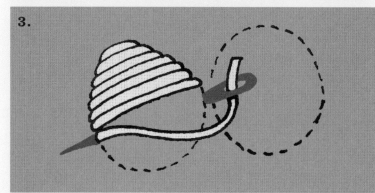

3. SATIN STITCH

The gingerbread man's cheeks (see page 87) are made of this. Stitch straight stitches very close to one another within the small area you want to cover, making the stitches longer or shorter as necessary

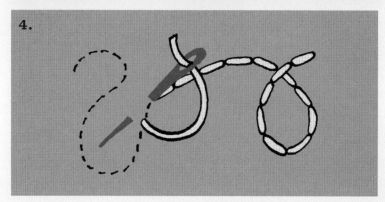

4. BACKSTITCH

Bring the thread through on the stitch line and then take a small backward stitch through the material. Bring needle back through, a little in front of the first stitch. Then insert the needle back into the fabric where it first came through.

using a sewing machine

You don't need a brand new machine, or one that has lots of different stitches and settings, to complete the projects in this book. If you are thinking about investing in a machine, it is often a good idea to go to a specialist machine shop to ask advice and try before you buy. Many of these centres will also sell secondhand machines and can service and recondition existing models. Straight stitches of various sizes and zigzag stitch are the only ones that are used in the projects, but if you think you might get hooked on homemade there are some machines that have a stitch setting for everything.

If you are new to sewing, read through the instructions for your sewing machine and ask the shop assistant for a basic tutorial on threading and using your purchase, or find a sewing friend to slowly explain the simple settings on your machine. Practise lots on old pieces of material and keep children well away from the needles, settings and foot pedals.

Make sure you understand about adjusting the tension, (the tightness of the stitches) so that you can select the right option for sewing through thick blankets or fine lace.

Learn how to thread your machine and wind the bobbin, too, and look after it really well. Regular servicing according to use helps extend the life of your machine.

SEWING MACHINE TECHNIQUES

Cast on by sewing a half centimetre or so of stitches, then backstitch back to the beginning. Now sew on along your sewing line. Repeat this at the end of the line to ensure your stitches don't unravel.

For fiddly areas, or where you are sewing over knitted fabric, use small stitches to secure the material firmly, and progress slowly.

Use zigzag stitch when you want to attach appliqués or ribbons to the surface of fabrics, and make sure that you remove pins just before you sew so you don't break your needle.

MADE
BY
HAND

apothecary bottles & decanter shampoos

There seems to be an almost never-ending supply of unwanted decanters of all shapes and sizes in thrift shops and at markets. Not all have their original stoppers but these, too, turn up regularly, or can be replaced by an old champagne cork. Internet auction sites are a rich source of old chemist's or drink bottles with stoppers that are the perfect size – just steer clear of any ridged, blue or dark brown glass bottles or anything with the words 'NOT TO BE TAKEN' impressed on the side, as they may have contained poison of some sort or another. Finally, if you can't find any of these, champagne bottles make a great alternative for this project.

1. When you have found a suitable bottle or decanter, give it a thorough clean inside and out. You can buy special decanter beads to swirl around the base to remove traces of old port or wine, but a handful of small smooth pebbles and a few soda crystals gently shaken around have the same effect.

2. Choose some pretty-coloured bubble bath, bath oil or shampoos to pour into the clean, dry bottles. Fill the bottles or decanter to the brim and close them with their stopper or a cork.

3. You can use melted sealing wax and string to form a really tight closure, or simply tie some ribbon or coloured string around the neck of the bottle and the stopper. Use a luggage label or tag and handwrite the name of the contents and any message on it, then attach it to the ribbon or string.

YOU WILL NEED:

a length of thick but pliable wire (garden wire is perfect) | pliers | ribbons and lace | reclaimed beads and baubles from vintage necklaces, old chandelier pieces, keepsakes or jewellery | strong thread

beaded door hanger

This item has an almost childlike simplicity, which looks very effective. It's a sort of charm bracelet for your door or anywhere else you'd like to hang it.

1. Begin by making a shape for the door hanger from the wire. Try hearts, simple house shapes or letters. Leave a little excess wire at each end so that you can secure the hanger when finished.

2. Then start to thread bits and pieces onto the wire. You can tie on little lengths of lace and trimmings, thread on large beads, use thread to attach strings of smaller beads and baubles, add buttons and any small trinkets of the right scale.

3. When you have covered all of the wire with interesting bits and pieces, hook the ends together and twist them into a loop. Add a length of ribbon for hanging.

YOU WILL NEED:

old suitcase, hatbox or trunk | cleaning materials | PVA glue | water | pasting brush | fabric for covering (choose whole pieces cut to the right size or little squares to patchwork over the surface) | craft knife or small scissors

little covered suitcase

Old baggage comes in all sorts of shapes and sizes. Many bags and cases still have shipping labels from their last journeys and some interesting clues as to whom they belonged. They were built to withstand robust handling as they were portered between boat, railway luggage car, cart or carriage, stacked high and packed full. As a result, many pieces are now battered and worn and often in need of some repair. Others have been left for ages in attics, and are in great shape, but could do with a little sprucing up. There are lots of different designs and finishes, from scuffed canvas to beautifully aged leather. The subtle tan leather cases and trunks should be left to improve with age, but from all the rest you can choose anything from the smallest cardboard child's case to the biggest steamer trunk to turn into a swanky new present.

1. Whatever type of luggage you choose, ensure it is structurally sound, opens and closes easily and has no sharp nails or hinges on the insides or outside. Begin by giving the case a really thorough clean. Start with the outside and any catches or metal. Remove any rust with some fine wire wool and oil the catches so that they open smoothly. Polish any wooden beading or leather corner supports with a soft duster and some beeswax polish.

2. Using a well-stirred mixture of two-thirds PVA glue and one-third water, paste the glue thickly and evenly onto the area that you want to cover. Then start smoothing on the little squares or whole pieces of trimmed fabric. It doesn't matter if any glue gets onto the surface of the fabric as it becomes clear when dry. When you get to the edges of the lid of the case, continue sticking all around the lip, gluing a little of the fabric to the inside of the case to keep it neat. Use lots of glue so the fabric is stuck firmly in place.

3. Glue pieces of fabric right up to locks and catches, then use a sharp-bladed craft knife or small scissors to trim off excess fabric around their edges. Leave the case open to dry.

4. When the glue has dried, repeat the process and do the same on the inside. Cut scallop-shaped strips of fabric for borders, stick on braid or even use old wallpaper or maps to decorate the inside.

5. Finally, you can stencil the initials of the lucky recipient onto the baggage, add a luggage label with your message, or fill the whole thing up with whatever takes your fancy.

layered cake stands

These are so effective and really very simple to make: the time-consuming part is collecting all the plates and glasses together. Old-fashioned tea and dinner services are full of plates and dishes that we don't use now. There are special dishes for bread and butter and muffins, stands to go under terrines and teapots, and countless different plates for each course of the meal. Incomplete dinner services and tea sets and pretty individual plates can be found everywhere and these lovely stands can be made of graduating-sized pieces, from two to about seven layers high.

You can use little liqueur glasses, candlesticks, bud vases, teacups, cut-glass pots or tiny shot glasses to sandwich between each layer. You can go for a totally eclectic look if you need a present in a hurry, or carefully rummage around shops and markets or your dresser to find a selection that are a match made in heaven. It is probably a good idea not to use any really precious pieces, as gluing together a whole set of early, hand-painted, priceless porcelain does not have quite the right preservation principles we should have in mind.

1. Decide how many layers you would like and assemble the plates you are going to use. Choose a theme, style, age or colour of plate, if you have time to plan the stand. A serving, main course, starter, side and tea plate from the same set make a really simple stand. Whatever plates you choose, arrange them with the largest first and gradually getting smaller, with something interesting to go on the top if you like – a teacup, sugar bowl or even a little vase looks lovely. Choose the glass stackers that go in between each layer and check that they all fit inside or outside the lip on the base of whichever plate they are to support, and that they have an even rim so you can glue all the way around.

2. Clean and dry everything really well. Place the first stacker right in the middle of the largest plate and use a wipe-off marker pen to draw a circle around the base of it. Turn the next plate upside down and stand the stacker on its head in the centre of the plate's base. Draw a circle around the rim of the stacker. Repeat this process with every layer of plate and stacker, so that you have all the positions of the pieces marked.

3. Then, starting with the largest plate, squeeze a plentiful, even amount of glue around the base of the first stacker and place it inside the marked circle. Make sure that you do not glue over the marker pen line or you will not be able to wipe it off when everything is stuck together.

4. Let each layer dry before attaching the next layer. Finally, finish the stack with a single plate or a teacup and saucer or vase at the top.

5. Make a box that fits the stand so that it can be transported safely. The finer the glassware you use, the more delicate the stand will be. Pile it up high with cakes, biscuits and sandwiches, or use it as a stand for jewellery, trinkets and baubles.

cheese plates

Even the most accomplished cook or perfect baker can dread the uptake of the offer of 'is there anything I can bring?' when asked to eat with friends. Despite a former life as a professional chef, I always seemed to spend the journey to supper with an apple pie on my lap that had burned whilst I tried to put the children to bed, dry my hair and fish out something vaguely acceptable to wear. I now cut to the chase with a simple 'should I bring a lovely piece of cheese?', which is normally very well received and can be accompanied by a little stack of ribbon-tied vintage plates.

1. Unmatched or 'harlequin sets', as they are sometimes known, are all part of the charm of making a collection like this. There are no hard and fast rules, but for a little bit of continuity, try to gather together plates that are either made from the same type of material or decorated in the same way, or with similar colours, or from a particular era. Tea plates, side plates and even the odd saucer are a good size to look out for.

2. Once you have selected your best stack, choose a pretty length of ribbon to tie them all together and pop a generous slice of your favourite cheese on top, wrapped in waxed or brown paper.

YOU WILL NEED:

cufflink findings or old reclaimed cufflinks | interesting beads, buttons or trinkets | instant gel adhesive | materials to make a drawstring bag (see page 105)

cufflinks

Bead shops sell some very reasonably priced cufflink findings that you can use, or ask in charity shops for any old cufflinks that are mismatched or can be recycled. There are two main types of cufflinks. One type has two pieces joined with links and the other has a front with a little bar behind to go through the cuff. If you are using the linked variety, make sure that at least one of the sides will still fit through the standard shirt buttonhole when you have added the buttons or beads.

1. If you are using reclaimed cufflinks, give them a good wash and polish before you use them.

2. Simply attach the chosen embellishments to the cufflinks using the adhesive and leave to dry.

3. Make a little gift bag for them if you wish. Follow the instructions for the advent calendar bags on page 107 to make a simple drawstring pouch.

fabric pictures

We have lots of empty frames on the walls of our house. Some are hanging in their own right as something beautiful and pleasing to see whilst others are waiting to fulfil their potential. I can never resist an old gilt frame, and the fact that they might come without a canvas gives the perfect opportunity to create a present.

Any solid wooden frame will do: make sure that whatever you find is strong and not peppered by old or new woodworm. Keep your eyes open for fabric of the right size or scale to fill it – flags, finely printed tea towels, vintage headscarves, fabric with big patterns and scenes, old embroideries or even old clothes look great framed up and hung high. There are masses of fabulous floral fabrics that you can use, or hunt down designs showcasing boats, winter scenes, cowboy images, or whatever will suit your lucky recipient.

1. Carefully clean up the frame on the front and the back before you add the fabric. Use a dry paintbrush to remove any old dust and polish the wood with a soft duster where appropriate. Check for old nails or tacks in the back of the frame and remove any that you find with a pair of pliers.

2. Cut a piece of card that fits snugly into the back of the frame.

3. Lay the frame over the area of the fabric that you want to see and chalk around the outside of the frame. Cut off the excess fabric along this line if the fabric is not too precious.

4. Put the frame face down on a surface. Place the fabric face down, in the frame in the position in which you want it. Use a staple gun to attach the top edge of the fabric to the rebate inside the frame. Gently stretch the fabric taut and staple it in place along the bottom edge, and then along the sides of the frame.

5. Tuck in the edges of the fabric (untrimmed if it is a lovely flag or scarf that you can carefully remove in the future), and pop in the piece of card and tape it in place. Add a ribbon or cord to hang the picture.

YOU WILL NEED:

bars of soap | pretty old wrapping paper,
vintage wallpaper, fabric or old linen
maps | string, ribbon, bias binding or ric rac

guest soaps

*I love neat little stacks of these soaps in the bathroom.
And somehow, even though I know exactly what is
inside, I still enjoy opening a new bar every time.*

*You can use any wrapping paper, old wallpaper,
out-of-date map or even fabric to wrap your favourite
scent and size of soap. Squares of handcut soaps work
well, or simply buy family packs from the chemist
or supermarket. Pretty ribbon, thick string or bias
binding all make lovely trimmings.*

1. Cut a piece of paper or fabric just large enough to fit around
   the soap. Place the bar on it and wrap it up like a neat present.
   Tie the ribbon around and knot it in a bow. Add a little tag with
   a handwritten note explaining which type of soap is inside if
   you like.

2. Wrap up lots of soaps in all sorts of different combinations
   and give them as little thank yous or bundle them together
   and pop them into a basket with some apothecary bottles of
   shampoos and bath oils (see page 27).

YOU WILL NEED:

patterned fine cotton vintage fabric (gingham or delicate flower patterns have the right feel) | paper for template | pencil | jars of jam, pickle, mustard, jelly or even sweets | plate or saucer | paper scissors | tailor's chalk | pinking shears | luggage label or stickers | pen | elastic band or stretchy hair bands | pretty ribbon

handmade jams & jellies

I think that everyone loves the idea of a well-stocked larder, an ordered pantry or a tidy cupboard. Making these classic jam-pot covers is a great place to start, and even if you are not a domestic goddess in the jam-making and pickling department, these pretty little frilly lids will have everyone convinced.

For the ultimate cheat, take a jar of really good-quality shop-bought jam, pickle or jelly, leave it unopened and carefully soak off the paper label and then dry the jar thoroughly before adding your own finishing touches.

1. Old shirts, aprons and napkins that are past their best are great potential sources of the fine cotton fabric needed for these lid covers. Make a paper template that is the right size for the jar you want to cover: usually the circumference of the lid plus 3–4cm all around is a good rule of thumb to follow. Use a small plate or a saucer to draw around.

2. Chalk around the template onto the wrong side of the fabric. Cut out the circle using pinking shears.

3. Using your best handwriting, copy down the ingredients, the name of the jam and the date the jam was made onto a luggage label.

4. Place the fabric circle over the jam jar and stretch the elastic band or hair band over it so that it is tightly pulled in to place. Add the ribbon and luggage tag. Pretend you made it all on your own.

pretty lamp

Handmade housewarming gifts that are really useful are always well received. These lovely lamps and colourful shades can be created to match existing colour schemes or as stand-alone pieces. Lamps, odd shades and the fabric to cover them can all be picked up for very litte at markets and thrift shops. Make sure that the electrics and fittings are of the modern type and take them to a lighting shop to be checked if you are in any doubt.

If you sew often, you will have lots of little scraps of fabric that are left over from various projects. Even the smallest inch of pretty fabric can be used to transform lamps, lampshades, trays and even whole pieces of furniture into something beautiful. Choose fabrics that go well together, or that share a similar background colour or design.

1. Trim the fabric scraps into little squares, with pinking shears if you like.

2. Paste the PVA glue onto the lamp base and then start adding the squares of fabric, one next to the other, to create a layered patchwork that covers the existing finish. Change the fabric every so often as you progress up the lamp and make sure that the pieces overlap each other slightly so that the whole surface is covered.

3. Add strips of ribbons, lace and cut out fabric leaves and flowers to the covered base by pasting them with lots of glue, and sticking them to the patchwork. When you have finished, paint a coat of PVA over the whole lamp and leave it to dry.

4. Choose a lampshade that has a taut, plain fabric finish, or one that is made of stiffened card covered in fabric. Cover it with a patchwork of fabric in the same way as for the lamp base, and finish the top and bottom edges with glued-on lengths of ribbon to make it look neat and tidy. You can also add some bobble trim in traditional lampshade style.

YOU WILL NEED:

plain cork notice board | paint or scraps of fabric for the frame | paintbrush or pasting brush | patchwork hexagon template (see page 168)| vintage wrapping and wallpapers | PVA glue | box of pushpins | gift tag

patchwork noticeboard

I have tried to make the kind of patchwork that I would like to own on a number of occasions. Not for me the simple machined squares; I hanker after minute hexagons of perfect chintz or faded ticking, cut from flannel shirts and best dresses, and all held together with meticulous stitching. But there is something about the perfect symmetry, incredibly slow progress and precision of the whole process that I understand I will struggle in vain to achieve. So I like to cheat. Paper, I have discovered, can be just as effective. The simple option is pictured opposite, but see page 169 for the patchwork version.

1. Paint the frame of the noticeboard. Water-based acrylics are easy to use for this as they are low in odour and you can wash pots and brushes in water. Or use PVA glue to stick fabric all over it in the same way as for the lamp on page 47. Wait for this to dry completely.

2. Then make the hexagons. Use the traditional patchwork template on page 168 and draw around it lots and lots of times onto the backs of several different wallpapers, wrapping papers, printed pictures, or even scraps of fabric, and cut them all out carefully.

3. Using PVA glue and a brush, paste the backs of the hexagons and stick them to the cork board. Push the pieces at the edges of the cork board underneath the wooden frame if possible, or trim them to fit perfectly. Work your way around the noticeboard, butting all the hexagons edge to edge until no cork is left showing.

4. Add a little box of pushpins and fix your gift tag to the board.

A STEP FURTHER...

You could also add a twine grid over the top to tuck notes and envelopes, postcards and reminders into. Use a staple gun to firmly hold one end of a length of garden twine in place. Stretch it across the board, stapling it in place as you go, weaving in and out until you have a mesh of evenly spaced strings. Secure the loose ends with staples.

SIMPLE OPTION

If all of this is too complicated for you, track down an old map and stick that to the noticeboard using PVA glue instead.

planters for christmas & spring

Teapots with no lids and biscuit tins, vintage vases and big teacups, little pudding basins and coloured glasses, sugar bowls and sauce terrines, Toby jugs and coffee pots, old enamel and bright, jolly jugs all make very useful pots to fill with bulbs and flowers. The odd chip or crack that means they are not suitable for their original use can be overlooked or covered with soil.

Choose your container and an appropriate-sized plant or bulb or handful of seeds. Tiny scillas and little snowdrops will flourish in an old glass, daffodils or hyacinths like the room a teapot offers, several primroses might squeeze into a vegetable terrine and even a sprinkle of mustard and cress will grow into perfect 'hair' in a Toby jug.

1. Pop the crocks or stones into the bottom of the container for drainage. Have a look at the guidelines for growing the chosen plant, then add the compost, bulbs, plants or seeds. Add the compost and before adding the bulbs, plants or seeds.

2. For bulbs and plants, top the soil with a little layer of moss, shells, pebbles or even buttons to make it look pretty. Water carefully, as there are probably no drainage holes, and grow on the plant until your little pot is ready to be gifted.

plate hangers

Sometimes I buy odd things and people (my husband) ask me why I have bought them. The answer that I nearly always have is that I want to hang them on the wall. So I have developed many different ways of hanging all sorts of things. Most useful for china plates (though probably not for your best Wedgwood or antique Spode) is to stick a length of ribbon loop to the back of the plate using instant adhesive. This transforms single saucers, lonely lids or pretty plates into wall candy and sweet compact gifts. Look out for the right sort of china at fairs and markets.

1. When you have found just the right plate, wash it and dry it really well. Then simply cut a loop of strong ribbon to the right length and stick it firmly to the back of the plate using instant adhesive. Make sure that you only stick the ribbon and not your finger to the plate.

2. Pull on the loop to test that it is really secure before you hang it on the wall. Add several loops for larger plates and only use pretty, not precious, pieces.

YOU WILL NEED:

old broken necklaces and jewellery, glittering trinkets, charms or baubles | scissors | pointed-nose pliers (optional) | reels of waxed cotton thread (available from beading and craf shops) | fine elastic thread | blunt needle | clasps (available from bead shops or reclaimed from vintage necklaces) | little glass jars or divided boxes that are less breakable for smaller threaders

beads & baubles kits

My children have always loved threading things and making special 'jewellery' that their teddies, themselves, their grannies and lucky me HAD to wear. After several trips to the shops wearing chokers of old cotton reels, and even some penne pasta threaded onto string, I started collecting up old beads and broken jewellery for them to use instead.

There is no shortage of old necklaces, beads and strings of mock pearls. Thrift shops often have boxes that are not on display full of beads, buckles and buttons that can all be re-threaded, and auction houses regularly have lots of mixed costume jewellery. Avoid the moulded strings of beads that have no holes running through their middles.

You might even find some real pearls or amber as you collect your hoard. Pearls have a gritty outer layer that you can feel if you rub them against your teeth. Amber beads, even though they look like polished butterscotch and feel like they may be made of plastic, will pick up little pieces of tissue paper. Should you find either of these, perhaps put them aside and save them for the kind of threaders who will appreciate a real pearl or an ancient piece of fossilised resin.

1. Collect up as many pretty strings of beads, mock pearls and necklaces as you can find. Wash them all carefully in some washing powder in plenty of hot water and dry them with kitchen paper.

2. Cut off any clasps that can be re-used and remove any pieces of thread that are still attached. Then unthread all the beads and discard any that are broken, chipped or no longer looking their best. Some bead necklaces used to be knotted, so you may have to cut in between each one to release them. You may need pointed-nose pliers for undoing the tiny loops that hold some jewels in place.

3. When you have a good selection of pieces ready for threading, you can group them into different sections according to colour, size, style or any other grouping that seems fitting. Pop them all into small jars or a divided tray and label them according to their style.

4. Add some reels of thick waxed cotton thread, some fine elastic threads and a blunt needle and any clasps that you have. Gather it all up in a basket or box for an ideal rainy day gift.

gifts for a weekend away

Invitations to stay the night – especially if you are going to be trailing several offspring, a barely trained dog or perhaps a new boyfriend – offer the opportunity to turn up with a basket full of brownie points that you can, no doubt, erode over the weekend. A pretty dessert for Friday night, some refreshing mint tea for breakfast, a little bunch of ribbon-tied herbs to help with supper and a stiff drink for your hosts after you have piled into the car at twilight on Sunday, might just secure your status as good house guests. Here are a few ideas for adding value to some vintage finds.

vintage puddings

Taking a course for dinner is always appreciated. Mentioning that you will be bringing it along is helpful. Have a look at the cheese plates idea on page 37, or make desserts your thing. A mismatched set of teacups or little glasses of each brimful of pudding, travel well and look lovely. Find out how many will be sitting down to eat and gather up the right number of little vessels. As a general rule, the smaller the glass or cup, the more intense the dessert should be. Search out your tried-and-tested recipes for suitable puddings – think syllabubs, mousses, jellies and pannacottas – or consider the ideas below.

* tiny liqueur glasses with brandy-soaked cherries and rich chocolate mousse

* bone china teacups filled with sherry trifles

* cocktail glasses filled with champagne and fresh fruit jellies

* little old coffee cups filled with tiramisu.

teapots & fresh mint

There are about two and a half centuries worth of teapots knocking around out there and the perfect ones that have some age are worth buying every time you see one. Accessorise the pot if you want to give it as a gift. If you are not a natural baker and a round of scones sounds like a nightmare, lay your hands on some mint from the garden or a big bunch from the shops, tie it in a little posy and hand it over with the teapot.

stiff drink

To create a lasting impression, you can leave behind a decanter of something delicious for your hosts to enjoy. Out of fashion for so long, decanters regularly turn up in thrift shops and at markets. If you have a choice, go for the hand-cut or heavy crystal versions. Fill them up with your host's favourite after-dinner drink. Whisky, brandy, Madeira, port or any fortified wine will keep well. Write out a little luggage label with your message and details of the contents.

wake up & smell the coffee

Old-fashioned hand-cranked coffee grinders are great pieces of vintage kit. Scour the internet for one that takes your fancy. They often have a little lever so you can adjust the coarseness of the grind. Look for the tabletop or clamp-onto-a-surface versions rather than the wall-mounted variety, as these bring the most instant satisfaction. Take along a big bag of rich, roasted coffee beans, in an old coffee storage canister if you have one, and you can guarantee a great cup of coffee to start the day.

teacup candles

YOU WILL NEED:

bone china cup and saucer | instant adhesive | two long, coloured candles | old saucepans | a couple of clothes pegs

Beautiful fine bone china cups and saucers used to be the only thing to be seen drinking tea from, and as a result there are plentiful supplies of incomplete tea sets, single cups and lonely saucers still to be found. I find it perfectly acceptable to mix and match saucers and cups of varying designs to make a harlequin set, but even then there are often a few odd pieces left over that can be used to make lovely candle holders. A little chip in the base of the cup can be overlooked for this purpose.

If you don't fancy using hot wax, simply stick the saucer and the teacup together with instant adhesive and pop in a tealight candle. The fine bone china positively glows when the candle is alight. You can also buy candle-making kits that include all the equipment and instructions for making your own candles, but a couple of coloured candles or the ends of several others are an economical way of getting just the amount of wax you need. The candle wax will not mix so well with your porridge, so it's better to find an old pan that is past its best and use it just for candle making.

1. Glue the cup to the centre of the saucer and leave to dry.

2. Melt the candles very gently in a small old saucepan inside another filled with water. The wax is flammable so it is very important that it does not overheat during this process, so do use this double-boiler method. Remove the wicks carefully from the molten wax: I fish mine out with one of the wooden clothes pegs.

3. Then pinch two pegs together with the wick in the middle and place them over the teacup so one end of the wick is nearly touching the bottom of the cup. Then gradually pour some wax VERY CAREFULLY into the cup until it is about three-quarters of the way up the teacup and leave it to set.

4. As it sets it will form a depression around the wick, so melt the wax again and fill in the surface so that it is level and leave it to set again. Repeat until the cup is nearly full and the surface is flat. Finally trim the wick leaving about 1cm above the level of the wax.

Candle caution: *As usual, wherever candles are involved, a sensible approach has to be taken when burning them. I don't usually let mine burn all the way to the end as, even though the cups are fired and will withstand reasonable heat, they may crack if in constant contact with the flame. And you should never leave a candle burning when there are no adults in the room.*

easter eggcups

Easter is all about eggs and, if making a fabulous Fabergé fake is out of your league, then tracking down a few gorgeous vintage eggcups might be the way forward. And because several generations before us were brought up to start the day on an egg, there is a varied and plentiful supply of eggcups in every thrift shop, market and car boot sale.

Choose your favourite cup, slip in lots of little eggs or one large one of the right size and finish by tying a ribbon around larger eggs. Alternatively, make easter trees by hanging decorated eggs onto pretty branches set in a container filled with pebbles, to hold the branches still, or create your own Fabergé masterpieces by sticking buttons, beads, velvet and jewels to polystyrene eggs from craft shops.

decantalabras

I once bought 12 decanters from our local auction house because they looked so pretty together. Their twinkly cut-glass facets caught the light so beautifully that I had to have them. Luckily there were no other bidders on the dazzling dozen that day, so I picked them up for a song and, once I had them at home, started looking for ways in which to show them off.

Decanters are regulars at markets, junk stores and charity shops, as no one has a sideboard these days to stand them on – or a desperate need for a pint of warm port to be on hand in the parlour – and, as a consequence, these glass beauties are often cheaply priced. They come in all sorts of shapes and sizes, but my favourites, which catch the light the best, are the hand-cut types. You can tell these from the moulded or pressed-glass variety as, when you run your hand over them, the edges and facets feel sharp and defined. Whichever style you choose, they all make lovely pieces to stand a candle in.

1. Clean the decanter really well: use a handful of smooth, clean pebbles or special decanter cleaning beads to swirl around on the inside and remove any traces of single malt or vintage port.

2. If you can, try and find some bobeche. These are the little glass cups that you find on candelabras, sometimes with cut-glass droplets hanging from them. Candle shops also stock drip tray saucers that look great, too.

3. All you need to do is buy a candle that fits snugly into the neck of the decanter, add the bobeche if you have one, and wrap it up with a few spare candles and the stopper if you have it. If you are feeling particularly creative, make a little garland of flowers to sit around its neck.

Candle caution: *As usual, wherever candles are involved, a sensible approach has to be taken when burning them. I don't usually let mine burn all the way to the end as the glass may crack if in constant contact with the flame. And you should never leave a candle burning when there are no adults in the room.*

button bracelets

These are perfect little gifts for big girls as well as little girls. The choice and colour of buttons that you use means these can vary from candy coloured childish to classy-mother-of-pearl cool.

Never throw a button away: hoard them in a tin and reclaim them from all those shirts and pieces of clothing that are too well loved to wear. Raid the tins in charity shops or even buy whole lots on line.

1. Gather up a little bowlful of buttons that look good together and would suit your soon-to-be-lucky button bracelet wearer. Thread your waxed cotton thread or chosen yarn onto a slim darning needle.

2. Start with a piece of thread that is twice as long as you would need for a bracelet or necklace. At one end, thread on a chunky button going through both holes in the button, then tie it firmly in place with three or four knots leaving a length of thread trailing from the knot.

3. The second button you add needs to have four holes. Thread the short end of the thread that is trailing from the knot through two of the holes, and the long piece attached to the needle through the other and tie them tightly together, ensuring that both buttons lie flat, side by side, and are not pulled up so that they overlap.

4. Then add all the rest of the buttons, threading the yarn through each button several times so that they are all secure and remain evenly spaced apart. You can add little stacks of buttons, beads and jewels, or keep things plain and simple. Keep threading until you have a length long enough for your bracelet or a necklace.

5. When you have reached the length that you are after, add another four-hole-button, threading through only two of the holes, then, leaving a couple of centimetres gap, add your last button and tie it securely in place.

6. To create a loop at one end to secure your bracelet or necklace, double back the thread and push it through the two empty places in the four-hole button to create the loop. Tie off the end and trim it down. To fasten the bracelet, hook the loop over the button that gives the best fit.

SEWN

BY

HAND

baby blankets

I have always liked the idea of knitting or crocheting a whole blanket, until I remember that anything more than a teddy bear's scarf is too taxing a project for me to actually complete. So, with the arrival of each new addition to our immediate and extended family, I have been honing my alternative baby blanket-making skills that rely on ready-made blankets.

There are three key criteria to bear in mind if you would like to make a little warmer for wrapping up baby: everything that you use must be super-clean and easy to wash, safe and free from buttons, loops or loose trims, and incredibly soft and comfy so that it doesn't irritate a baby's delicate skin.

Merino blankets are the perfect material for this project, and nearly always have a thick, satin ribbon border that babies love to touch. Pick a blanket of a suitable colour; helpfully there seem to be lots of lovely duck-egg blue, rosy pink and pale cream ones that suit most nursery colour schemes. These blankets are also favourites with moths, so many have a few holes but are ideal for cutting up and re-using. Launder the whole blanket carefully on a wool wash with a baby friendly washing powder, and dry and air it well.

1. Decide on the size you want the blanket to be – a tiny one for a Moses basket, or bigger for a cot or bed. Measure out and mark with tailor's chalk the size of the blanket, using the ribbon-bound end or finished edge of the blanket, if it has either, for the top edge. You can choose from a straight or scalloped pattern

YOU WILL NEED:

tape measure | large merino wool blanket | tailor's chalk | fabric scissors | small plate or saucer to use as a template for the woollen scalloped edge | embroidery needle | various colours of embroidery or wool threads | letter templates (optional) | pins

for the blanket edges. For a straight edge, simply cut along the chalked lines using a pair of good sharp scissors. For a scalloped edge, use a small plate or saucer to chalk a scallop pattern along the three edges of the blanket that are not bound with ribbon. Cut along the scalloped outline.

3. The three cut edges now need to be finished with blanket stitch to stop them fraying. Choose wool or cotton embroidery threads in one contrasting colour, or many complementary colours, to blanket stitch around the newly cut seams. Blanket stitch is quite straightforward (see page 21 for instructions) and satisfyingly swift to whip around the edges with. If you are new to sewing, a thread the same colour as the blanket will disguise any uneven sewing.

Start at the satin ribbon edge and sew a couple of little stitches to secure the thread securely before you begin.

Sew along the three cut sides of the blanket, keeping the stitches at right angles to the edge of the blanket, so they create a fan shape around the edge of each scallop. If you need to start a new length of thread, or want to change thread colour, finish the thread discreetly on the back and start the new length with as little break in the pattern as possible.

4. You can add some initials or a name to the blanket if you wish. Use some of the blanket offcuts, or fabric of a similar weight, and cut the initials or name from it. Make the letters quite fat and not too small. If you need a template, choose a font and print letters in large size on a computer. Pin the fabric letters to the corner of the blanket and, using blanket stitch as for the edging, sew all around the outside of the shapes. Remove the pins and press.

christmas stockings

There is something really special about hanging out stockings at Christmas time, and one that is roomy enough for the most wished-for present makes a great gift in itself. You will need quite a large piece of thick woollen fabric, so an old blanket is perfect. Choose a plaid picnic rug, complete with tassels, or a thick bed blanket, often found with a satin ribbon edging.

You can make these special stockings as simple or as fancy as you like. Adding initials or names is both decorative and always good for avoiding any confusion in the early hours of Christmas morning, or you can just use a simple bauble design or pocket to embellish the stocking.

1. Start by making a template: have a look at the stocking in the picture, or copy one that you have already. Draw it out freehand on a piece of newspaper or, alternatively, draw around the biggest pair of Wellington boots that you have in the house and then add quite a few centimetres all around. Cut out the shape.

2. Blankets are perfect for this project as they have a helpful finished edge already. If the blanket is different on the front and the back, place it right-side down. Pin the top of the stocking template along the fringed or finished edge of the blanket and chalk around it to make the sewing line. Remove the template and cut out the stocking shape about 2cm outside that line. Turn the template over, chalk a mirror image of the stocking shape on the blanket and cut it out in the same way.

3. If you want to add appliqué decorations to the stockings, now is the time to sew them on. Simplicity is best, so choose strong Christmas shapes such as baubles or gifts, or the stocking recipient's initials or name, and cut them from vintage fabrics or felted wool. Or cut pocket shapes from more of the blanket and sew them to the stocking to hold extra-special little presents.

4. Pin the appliqués in place, ensuring they do not stray over the sewing line or they will disappear into the seam. Either hand-sew all around the edges with blanket stitch (see page 21), or machine-sew them on using the zigzag setting.

5. When you have finished the appliqué, place the stocking shapes right sides together, making sure that the fringed or ribbon-edged tops are level with each other. Pin the stockings together and then sew all around the chalk sewing line using backstitch (see page 21).

6. Turn the stocking right side out and trim off any excess seam allowance. You need to add a loop of ribbon to the top so that it can be hung up. Press open the back seam at the top of the stocking with a warm iron. Pin the ends of the ribbon loop across the seam allowances and sew them in place using backstitch on the machine or some good, strong handstitches.

7. You can sew a pompom to the tip of the stocking toe, and sequins, buttons and trims to the top edge if you have used fabric without a finished border, or just want to add a bit more sparkle.

YOU WILL NEED:

compasses | paper for template | paper scissors | little scraps of fabrics, from 3-10cm square | tailor's chalk | fabric scissors | pinking shears, if you have them | hand-sewing needle | sewing thread | pretty button

layered corsages

These are little stacks of different fabric circles, sewn together to form a layered flower. They can be made from tiny scraps of leftover fabric and transformed into lovely gifts with all sorts of uses. Once you start making these flowers, you will not want to stop. As you only need tiny circles of each different fabric it is often worth making several flowers at a time.

Rifle through your scrap bag, your too-small children's clothes or vintage fabrics and pick out some suitable materials. Some thicker pieces are always good to add some structure to the flowers. Use old blanket off-cuts, felted woollen jumpers that have accidently (or otherwise) shrunk during washing, velvet, lace, cotton and prints in plain and pretty patterns.

Make lots of flowers and string them along some narrow ribbon to make a little flower bunting, or use them as a pretty topper when wrapping a present.

1. The corsages need not be too regular, but if you need a template, cut out six or seven paper circles of gradually reducing sizes, from about 10cm down to about 3cm. Chalk around these templates on the backs of the different fabrics.

2. Cut the circles out using pinking shears or plain scissors; scallop some of the edges for a little contrast if you like. Pile the circles all on top of one another, starting with the largest at the bottom. Add cut-out leaf shapes or actual flowers from printed fabrics for variety. Swap the fabrics around between flowers until you have your perfect flower.

3. Sew a few stitches straight through the middle of the corsage to hold all the layers in place. Choose the best-looking button to top this little stack and sew it securely through all the layers of fabric onto the front of the corsage.

BROOCH

For a pretty flower brooch, simply sew a large safety pin into the middle of the back of the flower, sewing through just a few layers of fabric.

HAIRCLIPS AND BOBBLES

Sew a little flower to the end of a hairclip or hair tie with a few firm stitches.

SHOE DECORATIONS

Use strong fabric glue or a glue gun to stick flowers firmly in place on the front of a pair of plain shoes.

BRACELET OR CHOKER

These look lovely if you can find glass buttons or beads to add a little sparkle to the flower centres. Cut a piece of velvet ribbon to the right length to go around a wrist or neck, plus 3cm. Turn over the ends by 1cm and hem them with matching thread and add a popper so that the bracelet or choker can be easily fastened.

Sew a little row of tiny corsages, old buttons, beads and sequins along the middle of the ribbon. Little pieces from chandeliers are really well suited, too, as they already have helpful holes at the top.

coat of arms

You don't need to have a family history stretching back to the Domesday Book to have a coat of arms. Take a look at heraldic symbols and images in books or on the internet before you decide on your own design. There are several basic shield shapes that you can use for the outline, and it is better to draw these out on paper and plan the whole design before you pick up a needle and thread.

As with traditional coats of arms, it is lovely if your design reflects your intended recipient's name or occupation. Divide the shield into quarters and fill each section with little trinkets or scraps that suit the knight you have in mind. Old badges, beads, buttons and braids, anything that has metallic thread, monograms, name tapes or old jewels all look great. Use an embroidery hoop to keep the background fabric taut while you embellish it, and securely sew on each piece using embroidery silks.

When you have finished you can make your design into a cushion or stretch it over a canvas.

1. Draw out the shield on paper using the template on pages 164-5 to guide you, and cut it out to make your template. Lay out all the pieces that you want to add onto it. Arrange and move pieces until you are happy with the plan. Take a digital photo as a reminder of what goes where.

2. Draw out the shield shape directly onto the right side of the fabric using tailor's chalk. (When you have finished your coat of arms, you can brush the marks away.) Define the outline of the shield and the quarters in running stitch (see page 21) or by sewing on beads or ribbons or quarters of different woollen fabric cut using the template. (You can use a sewing machine to put these background pieces in place if you wish.) Then put the shield into an embroidery hoop to make the rest of the process easier.

3. Sew on all the other pieces that you have collected until the whole of the shield is bristling with reclaimed bits and bobs. Use embroidery silks and simple stitches to add detail in any blank areas or to sew initials, names, dates or mottoes into your design. Have a look at page 21 for a guide to simple sewing stitches.

4. You can cut out the finished shield and hand stitch it to a cushion cover or staple the finished fabric into a suitable frame for hanging.

YOU WILL NEED:

hard backed diary | ruler | paper for template | pencil | paper scissors | blanket or tweed fabric | tailor's chalk | tapestry needle | woollen embroidery threads or fine wool | pins | 2 lengths of ribbon

fabric diaries

Diaries and journals, address and visitor's books, cuttings and recipes, files and boxes all look so much easier on the eye with the addition of pretty fabric covers. There are a couple of quite simple methods that you can use to turn diaries into lovely gifts and plain notebooks into a handbag essential.

For diaries, loose covers make the best presents as they can be recycled with a new diary slipped into the same sleeve next year. Thick, hard-wearing tweed or woven wool blankets are the best fabrics to use, so keep an eye out for kilts and coats that might be suitable. Welsh blankets and reclaimed cloth from picnic blankets look lovely, too.

Be aware when you are making this cover that if it fits snugly when the book is open, it will be too tight when the book is closed, so check before you sew.

1. Measure the height and width of the diary when it is closed and then make a template half a centimetre taller than the diary and nearly four times as wide as the book when closed.

2. Pin the template to the wrong side of the fabric and draw around it with chalk. Cut out the shape.

3. Place the middle of the fabric against the spine of the diary and wrap the fabric around it, folding the extra fabric inside the front and back covers. Trim off any excess fabric if these inner flaps extend too close to the spine. Use chalk to mark exactly where the folds are. Then unwrap the diary and start to sew.

4. Thread up the needle with a length of embroidery thread or wool and embroider initials or a name, or sew a simple shape, such as a heart, to the panel that will be the front of the diary.

5. Fold the cover back into the right shape, using the chalk lines as a guide, and pin the inner flaps to the front and back panels along the top and bottom. Use blanket stitch (see page 21) to sew the top and bottom seams, sewing through both layers of fabric. Make sure that the diary fits snugly inside its cover and can be fully closed before you sew up the second side. Use blanket stitch to sew along the raw edges of the inner flaps to make them neat and tidy.

6. Sew on a couple of lengths of ribbon just inside the middle of the sides of the cover that can be tied together to hold the diary closed.

notebook

You can buy a whole range of plain and lined notebooks. Choose one that looks like a paperback book, not one with a spiral binding and some suitable cotton fabric. You can also use old linen backed maps or wallpaper, and follow the same method for a different vintage look. This is a two-stage process, so don't try to make everything neat straightaway.

1. Open out the book and press it down flat on the wrong side of the fabric. Chalk around the outline and mark out exactly where the spine is. Cut the fabric approximately 5cm larger on all sides than the book outline.

2. Spread a thin layer of PVA glue over the whole of the back, front and spine of the book. Press the book down within the chalked outline and smooth the fabric carefully over the cover, removing any air bubbles or creases. Close the notebook and then leave it to dry with all the edges of the fabric still sticking out beyond the sides of the book.

3. When the glue is fully dry, make a couple of scissor cuts right up to the edge of the book where the spine is. Either fold the tab that you have made into the spine, or cut it off neatly if there is no gap to tuck it into.

4. Mitre the corners by cutting across the fabric at a 45° angle at the corners of the notebook. Make the cut as close to the corner as possible without cutting the cardboard cover. Fold the flaps of fabric over to the inside of the cover and check that they lie flat and that the corner is neat. Spread a thin layer of PVA on the fabric flaps and stick them to the inside cover of the book.

5. Add a length of ribbon for a bookmark by gluing it firmly in place next to the spine.

6. Stand the book up and peg the pages together, leaving the covers propped open – or slide tin cans between the covers and pages – to stop the inside pages sticking to the fabric while the glue dries.

EMBELLISHMENTS

If you want to personalise your gift you can cut an initial or monogram from a contrasting-coloured fabric and stick it to the front of the book using PVA glue. The glue will become clear when dry, so don't worry if you get a little excess on the fabric at any time.

christmas decorations

There are so many customs and traditions associated with Christmas, so much excitement, unwrapping and decorating, that it is the perfect occasion for which to be making something special – a gift that will be kept and cherished for years to come, that can be stored away carefully. Hanging this festive selection of decorations, made from recycled and vintage materials, can become a tradition all of its own. The decorations don't have to be made from old or reclaimed fabric, but look lovely if you can find a few vintage pieces to work with.

gingerbread man

You need to use a thick, felted wool jumper or blanket fabric for this jolly gingerbread man. Choose plaids, Fair Isle or self-patterned fabric for any clothes.

1. You can trace and use the template on page 163, or draw around a gingerbread man biscuit cutter of the right size to create a template. Pin the template to the back of the fabric and draw around it with tailor's chalk, drawing two shapes for every gingerbread man you want to make. Cut out the shapes and then place them right sides out to create a double-sided gingerbread man.

2. Use blanket stitch (see page 21) and a contrasting colour embroidery thread to sew around the outside of the figure. Start at one hand and sew nearly all the way around the outside to the shoulder nearest the starting point, leaving just a little gap unseen.

3. Then, using the top of a pencil or the blunt end of a knitting needle, push a little stuffing into the gingerbread man until he is gently puffed up – a little padded figure. Now continue the blanket stitch to close the gap and fasten off neatly.

4. To add a loop to the top of the head, sew on a couple of loose stitches to form a loop and then knot the ends to secure.

5. Use dark embroidery thread to embroider two eyes, eyebrows, nostrils and a mouth in backstitch and running stitches, and red thread to embroider the cheeks in satin stitch (see page 21). Sew on a row of small buttons or beads down his tummy.

6. Use scraps of vintage fabric to add any other details you like, such as pockets, waistcoats or trousers. For any clothes, cut out the shape from the fabric and sew it directly onto the figure. Or just tie a ribbon bow around the gingerbread man's neck.

7. If you wish, you can fold the hands to the front and sew them together so that he can hold something, such as a little present or a bunch of holly.

clothes peg christmas fairy

1. Start by pasting some glue on the head of the peg and sticking on a circle of fabric to cover the top.

2. Cut a piece of fabric to make a cloak, scrunch up the top and hold it to the neck of the fairy. Tie on a coloured piece of embroidery thread or wool and wind it around the neck several times to hold the cloak in place. Then lift the cloak up and continue to wind the thread down along the body to the waist. You can change thread colours as you work if you want to.

3. Cut a length of lace for the skirt and work a line of running stitch (see page 21) along the top edge using embroidery thread. Pull the stitches up to make a ruffle and wrap it around the fairy's waist. Wind the thread around over the top of the lace to hold the skirt in place. You can layer more than one ruffle to make a very full skirt. Tie the thread to itself a couple of times and thread the end into the windings to secure it. Starting under the skirt, wind more embroidery thread around the tops of the legs to make a pair of knickerbockers for the fairy.

4. Cut some simple wing shapes from the lace or doilies and sew or glue them to the back of the cloak.

5. Cut some short lengths of embroidery thread or wool for the hair and glue or sew these to the top of the head.

6. Draw some eyes, two tiny dots for the nose and a little rosebud mouth onto the face. Glue on the ring, or a circle of threaded beads, to make a crown.

7. Peg your fairy to the top of the tree or suspend her with a loop of black cotton tucked under her cloak.

christmas pudding baubles

1. Begin by wrapping the fabric around the bauble and tying it tightly around the base of the hanging fitting with some embroidery thread. Trim off the excess and then stitch across the fabric until it tightly covers the bauble. Make a few stitches to secure it and fasten off.

2. Thread the ribbon through the hanging fitting in the top of the bauble and tie it to create a loop. Cut a circle of lace or crochet from a doily and scallop the edges. Make a little hole in the middle large enough to fit around the hanging fitting on the bauble (some crochet helpfully has a little circle in the centre where it is started from).

3. Place the crochet over the top of the bauble – pulling the hanging loop through the hole in the centre – and sew the crochet in place with small stitches through the wool fabric. Sew on the holly leaves and the beads.

fir cone garland

1. Cut a length of twine or wool as long as you want the garland to be. Make a little loop at one end for hanging it.

2. Thread on a couple of beads, bits of jewellery or baubles, tying the string in a knot between each item to keep the spacing as you want it. Then squeeze a big spot of glue from the glue gun or a tube of glue onto the fir cone and press it onto the twine. Press a bow or little scrap of crochet onto the glue as well and hold the elements together until the glue dries.

3. Keep going along the length of the twine, spacing out the beads, cones and any other little embellishments that look festive along the way. Finish up with another hanging loop at the other end. These garlands look fabulous on the tree, hung across the room or over a mantelpiece or frame (see page 85).

patchwork baubles

These can be made by simply sticking little scraps of fabric to a bauble with PVA glue. Patchwork the pieces on using lots of glue until the entire bauble is covered. Cut out a little circle with a hole in the middle and glue it on like a pretty collar at the top of the bauble. Thread a ribbon through the hanging fitting to hang the bauble on the tree.

mother's day sewing basket with pincushion & needle book

Everyone used to know how to sew, knit, crochet and embroider, and everyone used to have a sewing basket to store all their paraphernalia in. To revive this lovely notion, keep a lookout for a good-sized basket, either one specially made for the purpose or a shopping basket-style wicker one to pack your gifts into.

There are heaps of old-fashioned but still really useful sewing bits to be had. Hunt down as many vintage sewing finds as you can: wooden mushrooms for darning, brightly coloured bias binding, knitting needles, ribbons, hooks and eyes, buttons and embroidery threads all turn up regularly in thrift shops and markets.

SEWING BASKET

Add a pretty cotton liner to the basket so that no fabrics or threads snag on the wickerwork.

1. Start with a whole sheet of newspaper. Scrunch it up and then flatten it out so that it creases more easily, then push it down into all the corners of the basket. Trim off all the edges that are sticking up above the sides of the basket. Use this paper as the template to cut out the fabric for the lining, adding a little extra all around the top for a hem.

2. Turn under the hem and iron it. Sew it all the way around using a sewing machine to speed things up if you like. Sew on a trim if you like (old lace, braid, bias binding or even the ruffle off an old pillowcase looks good), or leave it plain.

3. Place the hemmed circle in the basket and, using a long needle and thick button or topstitch sewing thread, sew the lining into the basket all the way around with running stitch (see page 21). You will need to look carefully to see where the needle can fit between the strands of wicker. Sew just under the edge of the basket, gathering the fabric up where necessary so that it is evenly pleated all the way around.

STRAWBERRY PINCUSHION

Almost too good to stick pins in, these sweet little fruits can be made just because they look so lovely.

1. Use little scraps of red velvet or wool from a felted jumper and cut out two triangles a little bigger than the size that you want the strawberry to be. Pin them right sides together and backstitch (see page 21) around two sides, taking a narrow seam allowance and making a rounded point for the bottom of the strawberry.

2. Turn the cone right side out and fill it with lots of stuffing, packing this in really firmly.

3. With a needle and red thread, sew a line of running stitch (see page 21) all the way around the top of the opening. Pull up the gathers tightly and make a few stitches across them to completely close the top of the strawberry.

4. Cut out a jagged-edged circle from green fabric to look like the leafy stalk at the top of a strawberry. With thick green thread, sew a loop in the centre of this so that you can hang the strawberry up. Sew the leaves in place over the gathers with small stab stitches and matching green sewing thread.

5. With a tapestry needle and thick yellow or green embroidery thread, starting at the bottom and gradually working towards the top of the strawberry make tiny stitches to look like pips.

LITTLE NEEDLE BOOK

1. Cut out three different rectangles of fabric to fold in half to make the book as large as you would it to be.

2. Then, using pinking shears cut a piece of fabric slightly larger than the pages to make the cover.

3. Pin the rectangles of fabric to the inside of the cover to make the 'pages' of the book. Use running stitch (see page 21) and cotton thread to sew them in place down the centre. Fold the book over along the stitched spine and press it. Pop a few needles into the pages.

YOU WILL NEED:

wicker picnic hamper | tape measure | long ruler | tailor's chalk | vintage fabric | fabric scissors | pins | sewing machine (optional) | hand-sewing needle | sewing thread | long needle | button or topstitch thread

picnic hamper

'Glamorous' and 'outdoor eating' are words that rarely go together. However, this hamper is a million miles away from Tupperware, tepid tea, and curly ham sandwiches.

1. You need to create a cross-shaped piece of fabric to make a liner for the inside of the hamper. Measure the base of the hamper first and then the depth. Using a long ruler and tailor's chalk, mark out on the fabric the rectangular shape of the base, and then add the four side panels. Add a second line 2cm outside the first one and cut out the shape along this second line.

2. Right sides together, pin one side panel to an adjacent one along the sewing line – the first chalked line. Repeat with each adjacent pair of seams to create a box shape.

3. Sew up the seams using backstitch (see page 21) or with a sewing machine to speed things up.

4. Place the fabric box in the hamper and smooth it into the corners. Use a long needle and strong button or topstitch thread to sew the fabric in place through the strands of wicker in each corner.

5. Around the top of the hamper, turn under the excess fabric level with the edge of the wicker to form a neat hem. Using the long needle and strong thread again, sew the hem to the hamper with running stitch (see page 21), again working through the strands of wicker.

ACCESSORIZE YOUR HAMPER WITH:

plates
teacups
glasses
cutlery
napkins
picnic blanket

You can add some seriously retro contents to the hamper, give it just the way it is, or go the whole hog and pack up a picnic for a party.

Trim napkins in pretty bias binding, gather up embroidered tablecloths, roll up a plaid picnic blanket and collect together a set of beautiful bone china. Source coloured glasses, pretty thermoses and tiered cake stands, too.

Try trifles in pretty cups, leafy salads packed into old tumblers, baby bottles of champagne, beautiful bread wrapped in linen napkins, ribbon-wrapped bundles of knives and forks and little paper twists of salt and pepper.

covered hangers & shoe trees

Every girl wants order in her wardrobe, and these hangers are as pretty as they are practical. You can add a lavender-stuffed heart made of the same fabric, or some fabric flowers, near the hook, too. Look out for the old-fashioned wooden hangers that have a hook that unscrews, as these are super simple to cover.

Whilst you are hunting down old hangers, keep your eyes open for vintage shoe trees. Internet auction sites are a good source if you cannot see them at a car boot sale. They have a toe-shaped wooden end, a flexible metal strip and a little ball at the other end and they keep the shape of soft shoes beautifully and are often prettily gilded, too. Bundle them up with your hangers and present them only to your best friends.

Hangers covered in shiny satin material, carefully ruched along the top seam and padded with layers of wadding, look lovely, but are the trickier ones to make. The simpler process of making the all-in-one version, made with offcuts of blankets allows you to cover a wardrobe's worth of hangers in no time.

SIMPLE COVERED HANGERS

1. Unscrew the hook from the hanger if it does unscrew. Using the hanger as a guide, cut a strip of woollen fabric that will fit snugly around the hanger.

2. Using pretty-coloured thread and blanket stitch (see page 21), start sewing the fabric into a narrow tube. Sew up one short end, then once you have sewn a little way along the length of the tube, check that the hanger just squeezes into it, then sew nearly all the way to the end. Slide the hanger into the tube with the seam at the bottom, sew up the other short end and fasten off neatly.

3. Find the hole where the hook fits into the hanger with the needle and make a little hole with the points of the scissors. Using blanket stitch again, sew a circle around the hole. Thread the hook through the hole and twist it until it is back to where it should be.

FIXED HOOK HANGER

If the hanger does not have a removable hook, sew halfway along the tube, then slide the hanger into it with the seam at the top. Pull the hanger cover taut as you sew past the hook and then carry on until you have sewn all the way to the end. Fasten off well.

RUCHED HANGERS

1. Cut the wadding into long thin strips and wind it around the hanger until it is neatly covered, bandage style, in a layer of wadding. Use a couple of stitches to hold it in place.

2. Then cut a strip of fabric that is deep enough to wrap around the hanger and about 30cm longer than the hanger. Turn under one of the long edges and press it flat.

3. Establish the centre of the fabric by folding the long raw edge in half and pinching a crease on the fold. Open the fabric out again and sew the pinched crease to the wadding at the centre of the hanger with a couple of stitches.

4. Then, working out towards one end of the hanger from the middle, ruche the fabric up a little and sew it in place with small running stitches (see page 21).

5. Keep going until you have scrunched up all the fabric and stitched to the end. Then repeat the process on the other side of the hanger.

YOU CAN ALSO...

Add a woollen lavender heart. Cut out two small heart shapes of the same size from woollen fabric. With the right sides out, sew them tightly together with blanket stitch (see page 21), sewing nearly all the way around the edge. Spoon in a generous amount of lavender, then complete the stitching. Add a loop of thread to hang the heart from the hook of a hanger you've made.

Or, make some pretty layered flowers like the corsages on pages 75-6 and sew those on around the hook.

Or go crazy and add bobble trimmings, buttons and beads but ensure these are the types that won't catch on clothing.

easy peasy lace trim choker

Delicate and very vintage looking, this lacy ruffle of a choker takes a moment to make. You can make shorter ones, too, to be worn as pretty cuffs.

1. Hem the ends of the ribbon and sew on some hook-and-loop fastening or several poppers to make an adjustable choker.

2. Lay the ribbon out, right side up, on a table and lay little pieces of lace of different lengths all the way along it. Pin them in place and then sew them to the ribbon by hand using small running stitches (see page 21), or with the sewing machine, removing the pins as you go.

3. Spray the whole choker heavily with starch and then press it flat for almost-instant jewellery.

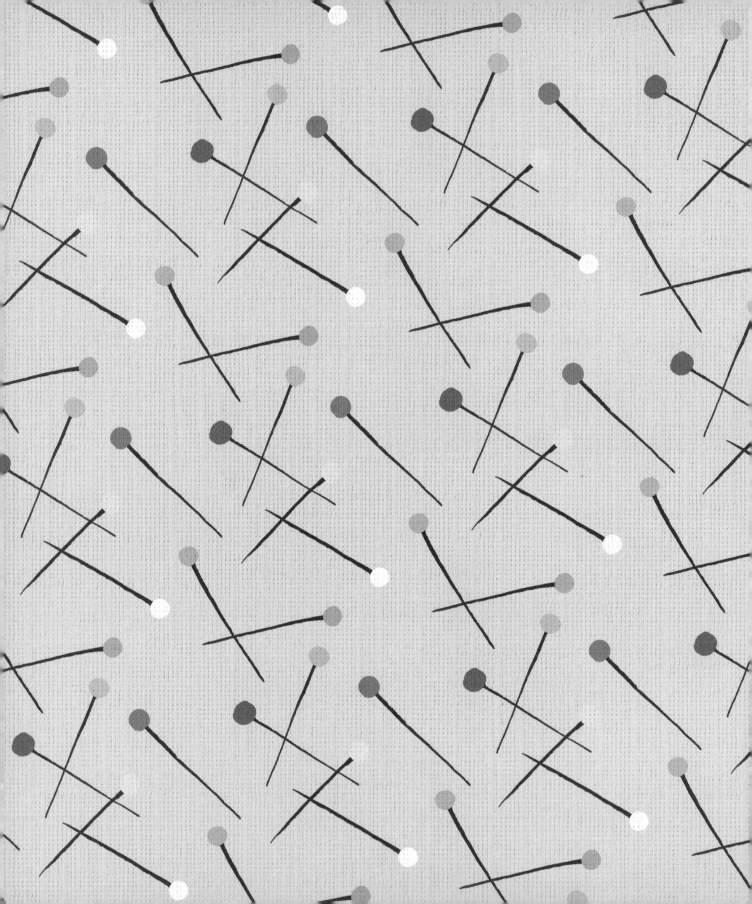

SEWN
BY
MACHINE

YOU WILL NEED:

lots of pieces of bright and beautiful vintage fabrics | tape measure | tailor's chalk | fabric scissors | iron | sewing machine | sewing threads | pinking shears | white cotton fabric | permanent black fabric pen | pins | thin string for the drawstrings | darning needle (long and blunt) | sweets, trinkets and treats to fill the sacks | old wooden frame | thick twine or string for the line, or length of ribbon, if hanging the calendar over a mantel | staple gun | mini pegs (available from craft shops)

advent calendar

In eager anticipation of the big day, children love opening these mini versions of Father Christmas's sack. Find an old frame, stretch some twine across it and peg out the little sacks for all to see. Make one large bag to keep the sacks in so that they can be safely stowed away for future festivities, while the frame can be used as a noticeboard for the rest of the year.

1. Measure, mark and cut out 48 little oblongs of fabric, each measuring 9 x 12cm. This might sound like a lot of pieces, but if you cut long strips from fabric that are the correct width (9cm) and then snip off pieces of the right length (12cm), it won't take long to cut them all.

2. Turn over a hem of about 1cm at the top of each oblong, press it flat and, using a small straight stitch, machine-sew it in place close to the bottom edge. You are going to thread the drawstring through this channel, so don't sew the ends closed. (Get a little production line going to speed your way through the process, rather than pressing then hemming one piece at a time.)

3. Using pinking shears, if you have them, cut out 24 white cotton fabric squares to write the dates on. Using the fabric pen, number them from 1st to 24th in your neatest writing. Sew one onto the middle of each of the 24 fabric oblongs with the machine, making sure that the hem is at the top.

4. Place the numbered fronts and plain back of the sacks right sides facing, ensuring that the top hemmed edges are level. Pin them together ready for sewing.

5. Taking a seam allowance the width of the machine's presser foot, sew each sack up from just below the drawstring channel, down one side, across the bottom and up the other side to just below the channel, then remove the pins. Leaving the channel free allows the drawstring to be threaded through from each side. Clip the corners off all the sacks, then turn all the sacks right sides out and push the corners out well for a neat finish.

6. To make the drawstring, thread the needle with the thin string and push it through the front channel and back through the back channel from the other side. Tie the loop in a secure knot and snip off the excess.

7. Fill up each little sack with sweets, trinkets or treats to make everyone in the house happy.

8. If you want to make a frame for the sacks, stretch pieces of twine tightly across the back of an old wooden picture frame, holding them in place with a couple of heavy duty staples from a staple gun. Use the little pegs to hang the bags along the tiny washing lines. Alternatively, peg the sacks to a piece of pretty ribbon and hang the calendar across the mantelpiece as part of your festive decorations.

christmas wreath

*Bows and baubles, tinsel and snowflakes;
vintage Christmas was such a twinkly, glittery
and unashamedly over-the-top affair that our
more recent pared-down, understated and
coordinated Christmas decorations suddenly
seem overly subtle by comparison. Have some
fun with this Christmas wreath and spread a
little vintage yuletide joy. Gather up as many
old-fashioned decorations and baubles as you
can find, or buy some bright little ones from the
high street. You will need a big bold, floral fabric
to help you out with the leaves and flowers, and
if you can bear the glitter drop, grab some glitter
and bring back the seventies sparkle.*

*Make the wreath in several stages so that
glitter and glue have a chance to dry.
This wreath is definitely for inside use only!*

1. First make the wreath base. On the back of the plain
   fabric, chalk around the large plate, then centre the
   small plate in the chalked circle and chalk around
   that, too, so that you have a doughnut-shaped outline.
   Make another doughnut shape and cut them both out,
   cutting 1.5cm outside the chalked lines. Pin them
   together with right sides facing. Set the sewing
   machine to a small straight stitch and machine-sew
   almost completely around both the inner and outer
   chalked lines, leaving only a 0.5cm gap in the same
   place in each circle.

2. At the gap, cut across the side of the doughnut,
   and then turn the whole ring right sides around.
   Stuff it really tightly with the polyester stuffing.
   Sew the gap closed by hand, tucking in the raw edges
   as you go.

3. Sew on a little loop of ribbon at the back to make
   a secure hanger.

4. Make flowers from the flowery-print parts of the fabric
   in the same way as the corsages on page 77. Cut out
   any leaves that are printed on the fabric, or just use
   green fabric to cut holly leaf shapes.

5. Collect together any baubles, beads, trinkets and
   vintage decorations for embellishing the wreath.
   Lay all the pieces out to make a pattern of how you
   would like the wreath to look. When you are happy
   with the arrangement, start sewing the pieces onto
   the padded ring or, for speed, use a glue gun. When they
   are all in place, add little touches of glitter, if you wish.

YOU WILL NEED:

template for bunny (see page 166) | paper scissors | pins | cashmere, merino blanket or reclaimed woollen jumper material | tailor's chalk | fabric scissors | sewing machine | sewing thread | dried lavender and millet (or polyester stuffing for younger bunny lovers) | small funnel or paper cone | paper to make bunny pattern | pompom for tail (steal one from pompom braiding) | embroidery thread or wool to make face and darning needle | hand-sewing needle and thread

lavender bunnies

A bad habit of shrinking precious wool and cashmere jumpers left me with a basket of perfect fabric to make my first bunnies. Full of remorse over the thickly felted, super-soft miniature versions of previously well-loved items of my family's clothing, I used them to make little bedtime companions for the children.

With simple embroidered faces, and lavender and fine millet-seed stuffing, they are ideal sleeping partners. The calming lavender aroma gets stronger as they are hugged and warmed up.

Bunnies can be made in any stretchy fabric, but I think that off-cuts from 100 per cent wool jumpers and merino blankets make the softest friends. Fine wool jumpers are better washed on a really hot wash so no stuffing can peep out through the knitted fabric. You can also use favourite too-small baby clothes or blankets as a precious keepsake of younger days.

The bunnies also look quite sweet holding something; a big carrot, Easter eggs, presents and flowers all look lovely. If you are making the bunny for a very young person, consider filling it with soft polyester stuffing so that it can be popped into the washing machine.

1. Make the template using the template on page 166. You can enlarge it, too, if you would like to make a bigger bunny.

2. Pin the template to the wrong side of the chosen fabric. Draw around the outside of the template using tailor's chalk; this will be the sewing line.

3. Remove the template and cut around the outside of the bunny at least 1.5cm outside the chalk line. Use the front as a template to cut a piece from the fabric for the back. With right sides facing, pin the two pieces together. Set the sewing machine to a small straight stitch and, starting at the right shoulder, sew all the way around the chalk line until you reach the base of the right ear.

4. Trim the seam allowance around the bunny, and cut right to the seam under the arms and between the legs. Carefully turn the bunny right side out (use a wooden spoon handle or the top of a pencil to help push the ears all the way out). Use a little funnel or a paper cone to feed a mixture of lavender and millet seeds (or polyester stuffing) into the bunny. Push it right down into the legs and into the ears with a pencil and pack as much filling in as possible.

5. Hand-sew the opening closed and fasten off the thread securely. Sew on a pompom for the bunny's tail.

6. Hand-sew across the arms, from shoulder to armpit, where they join the body using running stitch (see page 21), sewing right through the bunny to give shape to the top of the bunnies arms. Sew the paws together if you like. Using embroidery thread or wool and a darning needle, sew on the eyes, nose and mouth using small freehand stitches.

BUNNY ACCESSORIES

To make carrots, turnip and radishes, cut a quarter-circle out of appropriately coloured blanket or wool fabric. Fold it in half and machine-sew up the straight edge. Turn the cone right side out and stuff it with lavender or polyester stuffing. Hand-sew the top edges together, turning the fabric in as you go to create a neat seam. Add a few felt leaves to the top if you want an organic-looking vegetable.

These bunnies also like their own sleeping bags and blankets and some even like dressing up, so you can be as creative as you like.

tapestry cushions

I am not sure that it is possible to have too many cushions. They can instantly alter the style of a room as the seasons change, from blousy summer pinks and greens to subtle winter tweeds and checks, and they remain a relatively low-cost way of updating a look. These cushions are made with reclaimed tapestry fronts and pieces of vintage blanket on the back, so they can be enjoyed from all sides.

You can, of course, stitch your own tapestry panels, but not everyone has the time and patience for that. However, fire screens, pictures, chair seats and cushions were all made from tapestry panels in the past, and there is still a plentiful supply of these embroideries to reclaim and make into plump feather-filled furnishing accessories.

1. The size of the cushion will be dictated by the tapestry panel, so choose a cushion pad that is about 2cm smaller all around than the panel. If you need to cut the tapestry, set the sewing machine to a tight zigzag stitch and zigzag along the inside of the cutting line before you cut, so preventing the stitching unravelling.

2. For the back of the cushion, choose a wool fabric that complements the tapestry. A piece of unblemished and non-holey fabric from an old blanket or tweed coat, or any thick linen, is perfect. Cut the backing to the same size as the tapestry panel.

3. With right sides facing, pin the fabrics together. Set the sewing machine to a small, straight stitch and sew around three sides of the cover. Turn the cover right side out and stuff with the plump feather cushion.

4. To finish, oversew the gap on the open side closed. Alternatively, turn in and hem the edges and sew a couple of ribbons to each side of the opening to tie the cushion closed.

dog & cat cushions

Don't think that four-legged friends have to miss out on vintage gifts. Having spent years being woken up by cheeky terriers trying to get onto our beds, naughty Labradors pushing us off our favourite armchairs and the cat sitting on top of the cashmere as it aired on the Aga, we know that our favourite pets like a few human comforts. You often find old wicker baskets at markets and in thrift shops and you can either make the cushion to fit in one of these, buy a new basket, or simply use the cushion on its own. If you are using a vintage basket, give it a good scrub and hose down first.

You can make the cushions out of any strong fabric that is not too pale and that can be popped in the washing machine. If you are using a blanket that has holes or worn areas, sew on patches and mend the holes before you begin. Make sure that you make the cushion big enough for your chosen furry friend to lie on comfortably.

1. You need to cut out three pieces of fabric for the cushion: one for the front, and two for the back. This allows for a back opening so the cover can be removed and washed. Decide on the size of square or rectangular bed that you need, add 1.5cm all around for seam allowances, and cut a paper template. You will need enough fabric to cut out the template almost two and a half times. Mixing and matching different fabrics is fine. Draw all the way around the template in chalk for the front of the cushion and cut it out.

2. Now place the template lengthways and fold it into three even-sized pieces. Cut off the end third and use the remaining two thirds to cut a couple of pieces to overlap for the back of the cushion. If possible use a piece of blanket or fabric that already has a finished edge.

3. Before you sew the pieces together, you can appliqué motifs, initials or names to the front of the cushion. Cut out your chosen details: a bone shape for a dog, a little fish for a cat maybe? Use contrasting blanket fabric or similar woollen fabric that has been washed on the hottest cycle and has become slightly felted: old woollen jumpers work beautifully for this. Pin the appliqués in place, not too close to the edges of the cushion. Using the zigzag stitch on the sewing machine, sew all the way around the edge of the shapes. Alternatively, you can blanket stitch the motifs in place by hand (see page 21).

4. Lay the front panel out flat and right side up. Lay the first back piece right side down on top of it, then the second back piece right side down, ensuring the two unhemmed edges are to the sides and the finished edges overlap in the middle. Pin all the layers together around the edges.

5. Using the straight stitch on the sewing machine and taking a 1.5cm seam allowance, sew all around the outside of the fabric pieces. The seam will be quite thick in places, because of the layers of wool, so take it slowly and use quite a large stitch. When you have sewn all the way around, turn the cushion cover right side out and press it flat.

6. If you would like to add extra decoration, little upholstery trims and tassels look great sewn to the seams and corners using embroidery thread and a tapestry needle. However, if your pet loves to chew, then don't add anything they are likely to pull off and swallow.

7. Finally, stuff the cover with a suitably sized cushion pad. Or you can make your own simple liner using the paper template to create a cotton bag, filling it with polyester stuffing and machine-sewing the open side shut.

YOU WILL NEED:

*pretty fabrics that go well together | tape measure |
fabric scissors | sewing machine | embroidery sewing
thread | hand-sewing needle | selection of beads*

hanging mobile

*These long strands of little hearts can be hung as
a mobile, hooked up at a window or tied to flutter
from lampshades. They are super simple to make
and you can try cutting hearts, circles, squares
and even simple butterfly and bird shapes from
the fabrics to create your favourite design.*

1. Cut out lots and lots of your chosen shapes in varying
sizes from 2-5cm. See page 167 for heart template.

2. Arrange them on a table in the lines that you want to create,
adding several layers in different sizes as you go.

3. When you have as many groupings as you want you can
start sewing them into strings. Using a straight stitch on the
machine, simply sew down the centre of each shape and feed
on a new one just as the machine reaches the edge of the last
one. Sew up and down the sewing line a couple of times to
create a strong little string. Fasten off at the end.

4. Then use embroidery thread and a needle to attach a loop
at the top of the string and a little string of beads at the
bottom to weigh each string down.

hat, scarf & mittens

They say that necessity is the mother of invention and this is certainly the case with this collection of warming winter wear. It helps if you have a good idea of the size of the person you are making gloves and hats for, but a lovely long warm scarf fits all.

For the ultimate luxury, try to track down some old cashmere jumpers or cardigans. The older they are, the better quality and thickness the wool tends to be, and you can cut around or mend any holes by sewing on a small patch or tiny flower.

HAT

For a matching set use the fabric from one felted woollen jumper. Make the hat from the back and front of the jumper, the mittens from the arms and use any other leftover fabric for the scarf.

1. Measure around your head and divide the figure by four. To make the template symmetrical, fold a piece of paper down the middle and mark the divided head measurement out from the fold. Then draw out half the shape of the hat that you would like. You can choose from Wee Willie Winkie-style, a beanie or a bobble hat. Cut it out and open the paper up to form the template.

2. You will need to use the bottom welt or finished edge of the jumper to make the edge of the hat, so that it does not fray. Pin the template to the wrong side of the jumper front or back, with the straight bottom edge of the paper along the finished edge, and chalk around the shape. Remove the template and cut out the shape about 1.5cm outside the chalked line. Repeat to make the back of the hat.

3. With right sides facing, pin the pieces together. Sew all around the side seams with the machine set to quite a small stitch.

4. Turn the right side out and you have an instant hat. Sew on a pompom bobble, bell or even a pair of little ears to decorate, if you wish.

SCARF

You can make these winter warmers as long as you like.

1. Cut all of the remaining fabric into same-sized squares, the width that you would like the scarf to be. Cut more squares from other jumpers of different colours to make a stripy scarf.

2. Sew the squares together by placing them right sides together and straight stitching until you have two long strips of the same length.

3. Pin the strips right sides together and sew all along the sides and across one end. Turn the long thin tube the

right way out: use a broom handle to push the end out if it is proving tricky. Turn in the open end to form a neat edge and machine-sew across it.

MITTENS

These mittens have a tab fur trim around the wrists for extra warmth.

1. On a sheet of newspaper, draw out a classic mitten shape with the thumb sticking out at the side of the hand, making it the size you want. Then make the wrist section a little extra longer, like old-fashioned evening gloves. Cut the template out and write 'A' on one side and 'B' on the other.

2. Open up the sleeves of the jumper by cutting carefully up the arm seams. On the wrong side of the fabric, chalk around the template to make two 'A' outlines and two 'B' outlines. Make sure that the flat top of the template is against the finished edge that was the jumper cuff, and leave a little space between each outline.

3. Cut out the four shapes just outside the chalk lines. Pair them up to make a left-hand and a right-hand mitten. With right sides facing, pin the pieces together carefully so that the finished cuff ends are level.

4. Using the sewing machine on a small stitch setting, sew all around the chalk lines, leaving the cuffs open.

5. Turn the mittens right side around and then hand sew on a double sided strip of fur to make a comfy trim. Make sure that this is quite loose, so little hands still fit into the mitten.

6. Package the mittens up with the hat and scarf in a neat little bundle and wait for the cold weather to give the gift.

hot water bottle cover

Everyone in our house loves a hot water bottle. The calendars and thermometers are not nearly as accurate at announcing the arrival of cold weather as the calls for hot water bottles at bedtime. As a seriously unaccomplished knitter, even a basic woollen cover made by hand is a project too far for me, so this simple cover borrows somebody else's knitting to achieve the same effect.

1. You will probably need both the front and back of the jumper to make this cover, because you need to use the welt or finished edge at the bottom of the jumper as the top edge of the hot water bottle cover.

2. Draw around the rubber hot water bottle onto a piece of paper. Then draw a rectangle all the way around this, about 2cm outside of any of the edges and the top of the hot water bottle. Round off the bottom corners to mirror the shape of the bottle and cut the template out.

3. Have a look at any patterns on the reclaimed knitting that you would like on the front of the cover, then pin the template to the fabric accordingly, with the top edge (where the cover will open) on the finished edge of the jumper. Chalk around the other three sides of the template, remove the template and cut out the cover front. Repeat for the back.

4. With right sides facing, pin the front and back of the cover together, making sure the two top edges are level.

5. Then, using quite a small straight stitch on the sewing machine, sew around the three edges of the cover, about 1cm inside the cut edges, leaving the top open.

6. Turn the cover right side out. Thread the narrow ribbon into the darning needle and, starting at the centre of the front, weave it in and out of the woollen fabric, just where the narrowest part of the neck of the bottle will be, until you have threaded the ribbon all the way around the cover.

7. Double fold and hem the ends of the ribbons so they are neat. Put a couple of stitches into the back of the cover through the ribbon so that it can't be pulled out.

8. Pop the hot water bottle inside the case, pull the ribbon tight to gather the neck and tie it in a bow.

lavender cushions & hangers

*It is nearly impossible to reinvent the lavender bag,
but it is lovely to make a unique one from antique
and vintage fabrics. Pack them with a mixture
of perfumed fillings, sew on little loops so they can
hook over clothes hangers or door handles, or make
them heart-shaped to give to someone special.*

*Once you get started, you can produce a satisfying
stack in a short time. I have been making them for
quite a few years and each batch reflects my favourite
fabrics at the time. The millet or wheat grains make
the bags heavy and substantial and lovely to handle,
too. Have a look at the clothes hangers project on page
98 for instructions for making heart-shaped bags.*

1. To make the bags, cut out square or rectangular front and back sections from pieces of vintage fabric. Make the fronts and backs from contrasting fabrics: pretty florals on one side and ticking on the other; velvet on the back and roses on the front; stripes and spots; cotton and wool... the choices are all yours. Cut lengths of ribbon to make hanging loops.

2. Pin the fabrics together in pairs, with right sides facing, and add a ribbon loop if you like. The loop needs to be sewn into the seam as the bag is made, so place the looped ribbon between the two right sides of the fabric with the ends sticking out beyond the seam allowance and pin it in place.

3. Starting at the end opposite the loop, sew all the way around using a small stitch on the machine, but leaving a 4–5cm gap along one edge.

4. Turn the bag right sides out and make sure that all the corners are turned out neatly. Mix the millet or wheat grains half and half with your chosen perfumed filling. Try dried lavender flowers, dried rose petals or a spice mixture of crunched up cinnamon sticks, cloves and star anise: the latter is great for winter. Push the mixture into the bags through a wide-necked funnel until the bag is overflowing.

5. Oversew the gap closed with tiny stitches in a thread that blends in with the fabrics.

laundry bags

These bags are super-simple to make and the towels look as if they were created just for this project, rather than recycled for it. Guest and hand towels used to be made from huckaback (a thicker, patterned-weave cotton or linen fabric) and there are countless examples to be found, many of which have lace edgings or embroidery details. Hunt down some examples that are in good condition for these laundry bags. The towels should wash beautifully and press well, too, so give them a good launder and iron before you start to sew.

As with any item that has long tapes or cords, keep these bags away from young children as there is a risk that they might put them around their necks or over their heads.

1. Start by deciding which side of the towel you want to have facing out – there is normally one side that looks crisper and neater.

2. Lay the towel flat with the right side up, and fold over the two short ends of the rectangle towards the middle of the towel by about 10cm. If these ends have lace trim, fold over that, too, but make sure that 10cm of fabric is folded over as well as the lace. Press the folds flat. Set the sewing machine to a small straight stitch and sew across each end about 2cm from the fold to form a channel to thread the tape through.

3. Fold the towel in half with right sides facing and match the hemmed folds. Pin the sides of the bag together, making sure that the folded-over fabric (now on the inside) is not caught in the pinning. Machine-sew up each side to just below the drawstring channel that you made.

4. Turn the bag right side out and press it. Cut two lengths of woven tape or ribbon to make the drawstrings. Pin the safety pin to the end of one length and thread it through the front channel from one side of the sack and back through the back channel, from the other side. Remove the pin, cut the tape if it is too long, and sew the ends together. Repeat this from the other direction. You will then be left with two loops that, when pulled, will neatly close the bag. Give these bags as gifts filled with lovely nighties, pairs of pyjamas, a packet of pants, or just as they are.

YOU WILL NEED:

fabric | tape measure | cold water dye, if required | iron | sewing machine | sewing thread | wide elastic measured to fit the girl's waist size | large safety pin | hand-sewing needle | buttons and embellishments, if required

little girl's easy skirt

This is about as simple as making clothes can be, and you can choose your scale, so you can make the skirt big enough for Barbie or as short as is nice for your niece. Have a good hunt for suitably pretty or patterned fabric, take advantage of any recycled fabric that already has a hemmed side or embroidery, or cut down an old skirt to just the right size. If you find some fabric that would look better in another colour, there are some really simple-to-use cold-water dyes available. White damask tablecloths that are no longer fit for the table look particularly good when dyed, as colour highlights the woven pattern.

1. You will need a rectangle of fabric about 10cm longer than the length you want the finished skirt to be, and wide enough to be gathered to make a flouncy skirt. Follow the packet instructions for the dye if you want to change the colour of the fabric.

2. Press the fabric first and turn over a narrow double hem at the bottom and a deeper one at the top of the skirt. Press them for a neat finish. If the fabric has an existing finished edge that is pretty, you can use that at the bottom of the skirt instead of a hem.

3. Hand sew or use the machine's zigzag stitch to neatly sew the bottom hem, and use straight stitch to sew the waist hem. Make sure that the resulting channel is wide enough to thread the elastic through.

4. If you would like to add any patch pockets, simply hem a square of fabric on all four sides, then sew it to the skirt around three sides.

5. Fold the skirt in half, with right sides facing, and line up the two raw edges. Starting at the bottom hem, machine-sew all the way up the side of the skirt using straight stitch, until you reach the waist. Stop short of the top so that you can easily thread the elastic through the elastic's channel. Secure the stitching and then turn the skirt right side out.

6. Hook the safety pin through the end of the elastic and shut it carefully. Push it through the wide waist hem, scrunching up the fabric evenly as you pull the elastic through. Make sure that the other end of the elastic doesn't disappear inside the fabric; maybe pin it to the skirt to be safe.

7. When the safety pin emerges at the other end of the hem, hand-sew the ends of the elastic together really firmly. Then turn in and hand-sew the last little section of seam at the top. Press the skirt. Add buttons or extra trimmings , like this lace edging, for decoration if you like.

re-rigged old boats

It is not just little boys who love these boats. Classic model yachts were sailed on village ponds or boating lakes in parks for generations. Models were made in all sorts of sizes which nowadays regularly turn up on internet auction sites. Those that require refurbishment are often inexpensive, and these are fine, as long as all the wooden masts are still in place.

Choose fabric for the sails that will suit the sailor you have in mind.

1. Give the boat a careful check to ensure there are no sharp edges or broken pieces. If it looks as if the re-rigging process might be tricky, draw a sketch of the way in which the miniature ropes work before you begin as a record.

2. If you would like to repaint the hull of the boat, rub it down all over with sandpaper and paint it your chosen colour: maybe consider a colour that complements the fabric you are using for the sails.

3. There are two ways of refurbishing the sails. If they are all in good order and the rigging is intact, you can simply sew the new fabric to the existing sails. To do this lay the boat down on a piece of paper and draw around the sails to make templates and cut them out.

4. Chalk around these templates onto fabric. If the sails have seen better days, you will need to carefully de-rig the boat and use the old sails as a template. Save all the little rigging pieces so that you can tighten the sails. Now sew new fabric to existing sails, cut the fabric out a little larger than the chalked outlines.

Set the sewing machine to a small straight stitch and hem the sails on all sides so that they are exactly the same size as the original sails. Turn the templates over and make more fabric covers for the other sides of the sails.

5. Pin the covers onto the sails and, using a needle and thread, sew all the way around the edges using small running stitches (see page 21).

6. If you are making new sails, make a template in the same way as above. Cut out a back and a front for each sail, cutting just outside the chalk line, and place the pieces right sides together. Using the sewing machine, sew all around the outside of the sails, leaving just a little gap, then turn the sails right sides out.

7. Sew up the opening that is left using the machine or by hand.

8. Then, using the old rigging as a template, sew and tie on the thick cotton thread to act as new rigging. Put the sails in place on the boat and re-rig it.

pencil rolls

This neat little roll is just great for the start of a new school year, for keeping together favourite pencils or even brushes and little tubes of make-up. You can add initials, name tags or button decorations if you wish, too.

1. Gather up the number of pencils that you have to pop into your finished roll and anything else that might be useful to add to your gift.

2. Mark out and then cut a rectangle of woollen blanket material that is taller than all of the pieces of stationary you have chosen and long enough to space out all the pencils, with about 10cm extra. If there is a finished hem on the blanket, use that on one of the longest sides.

3. Then, on the inside of the roll, lay the three pieces of ribbon across the width of the rectangle and pin them in place, ensuring that all the pins are clear of the edges of the blanket.

4. You now need to neaten the sides around the roll. Turn over all the unfinished edges and make a hem about 1cm wide. Pin them in place, press and then use zigzag stitch to sew them down. The ends of the ribbon should be hidden under the hem.

5. Then, using straight stitch on the machine, sew up and down in lines at 90° to the ribbons to create tubes that are wide enough for the pencils to slip into.

6. Finally, fold the piece of narrow ribbon in half and machine sew it to the centre of one of the short edges to make a tie. Hem the unfinished ends, too, with the machine.

Add buttons if you like to decorate

When you have finished, pop the pencils and other little bits of stationery in, roll it up towards the ribboned side, wrap the ribbon around the roll and tie the ribbon in a bow.

YOU WILL NEED:

apron: *sheet of newspaper | pencil | paper scissors | one old shirt: big enough for the front panel of your apron | tailor's chalk | fabric scissors | strong woven tape or ribbon for the apron strings | pins | cotton for sewing | scissors*

baker's apron & biscuit mixture

Aprons are a great place to start if you have not sewn much before. I love these fabric ones as they can pop straight into the washing machine when your little cooking helpers have iced their cakes or baked their biscuits.

You can use any type of material that will wash easily. Make good use of reclaimed fabrics from clothes that already have buttons or pockets attached.

SHIRT APRON

With a little careful pinning and cutting you can make old cotton shirts a really helpful part of these aprons. You can make these for adults as well as children, so choose large man-sized shirts for bigger cooks, or smaller ones for the little chefs. Do up all the buttons and then reclaim the fabric by cutting along the main seams so that you are left with a front, back and arms. Use the front panel with buttons for your apron back and the back of the shirt for the front of your apron and save the rest for other projects. Mix and match shirts to create a double-sided apron.

1. Draw around an apron that you have of a suitable size. Alternatively make a template out of newspaper: cut the newspaper to the width that you want your apron to be. Fold it in half lengthways and sketch out a curved line across the top corner to make the shape of the bib. When you think that you have the right shape, cut through both layers of the newspaper and open up your template.

2. Chalk around the template on the reverse side of your fabric, then cut out the shapes cutting about 5cm outside the chalk line. Then cut the lengths of tape or ribbon for the apron strings: a good-sized loop for the neck and two long ties.

3. Place the back of the apron right side up on your working surface, then pin the apron strings in place, use the picture of the apron to the right as a guide, ensuring that all your pins are just clear of the sewing line. The loose ends of the loops and strings need to be pinned into the middle of the apron, well away from the sewing line, so they don't get caught up as you sew. Then place the buttoned front of the shirt onto the apron back, with right sides together, and pin them together too. Now sew carefully all around the sewing line.

4. All you now need to do is remove any pins inside, undo the buttons and turn the apron right side out, pay particular attention to the corners, so that they are nice and neat. Do up the buttons and you have a neat double-sided apron. Iron it for that crisp looking finish.

BISCUIT MIXTURE

Help your little chef along the way by adding a ready measured recipe for biscuits or perhaps a cake! Write out the whole recipe on a luggage label tag, making it clear what fresh ingredients need to be added.

Carefully measure out all the dry ingredients. Pour them neatly into a jam jar, using any currants, chocolate or spices to add layers of colour.

You can also fill tiny spice jars with icing sugar, baubles or little sweets to decorate the finished biscuits or cake.

Finish each of your jars with a circle of vintage fabric, cut with pinking shears if you have them, and secured in place over the top of the jar with a length of ribbon or string. Add the luggage tag recipe, too, and any biscuit cutters, if you can find them.

VINTAGE ACCESSORIES

There are some really useful baking accessories that you can collect to go with your aprons: keep your eyes open for old-fashioned pudding and mixing bowls, small rolling pins, old cookery books, biscuit cutters, wooden spoons, icing sets, little graters, measuring jugs and tiny tins.

SUGGESTIONS FOR MIXES

Massive jar with Christmas cake recipe and little pot of edible Christmas decorations.

Scones mixture with a little jar of jam and a round cutter.

Gingerbread biscuit recipe with a man-shaped cutter, raisins for eyes and icing mix.

Bread mixture and a tiny tin with little jar of seeds to go on the loaf.

Victoria sponge recipe with little jars of jam, icing sugar and baubles.

Biscuit mix with lots of chocolate chips and nuts.

tea cosy

I love a good cup of tea and have more than my fair share of teapots, most of which have their own bespoke jacket. I think you need to be choosy about your cosy. Not for me a shapeless acrylic knitted number, but rather a luxury cashmere snug-fitting, couture cosy.

As I am not a knitter I have to track down fine jumpers and scarves that can do the job for me. Vintage cashmere seems far superior to most of the current high-street offerings, so always pick up anything you see with an old-fashioned-looking label.

You need to use the welt of the jumper as the bottom edge for the cosy, so that you don't get unravelling wool straying into the tea.

1. Lay down the teapot with lid down on its side on a piece of paper and draw roughly around the body of the pot, excluding the spout and handle. Then remove the pot and draw a rectangle around the shape about 2cm clear of the pencil marks on all sides. Cut out the template.

2. Pin the template onto the woollen material, with the finished edge of the fabric lined up with the bottom of the template. Draw around the sides with tailor's chalk and then repeat for the back of the cosy. Cut out both pieces.

3. Then use a zigzag stitch on the machine to sew right along the unfinished tops of the woollen rectangles to neaten off the seams that will be the ruffle on the cosy.

4. Pin two sides of the cosy together with right sides facing, making sure that the top and bottom edges are level.

5. Use tailor's chalk to mark the height of where the spout and handle will be, and use a small straight stitch on the machine to sew up the sides at the top and bottom.

6. Turn the cosy right sides out. Then use a darning needle and woollen thread to add a line of wide running stitches (see page 21) each about 2cm below the top zigzagged edge. When you reach the end, pull the thread tight and tie the two ends securely together to form the ruffle at the top of the pot. Trim the ends.

7. Now you can decorate the cosy. Use little flowers cut from felt, fabric or blanket offcuts. Or add old buttons and trimmings, or embroider initials, a date or message. Turn up the base of the cosy, too, if it makes a better fit.

If all of the above is a little complicated, keep your eyes open for knitted bobble hats. Give them a good wash and then cut a couple of slits in these to push through the handle and the spout. Carefully hand-sew a little hem around the openings for an instant tea cosy, and pack it up with a teapot and a box of best tea.

doll's vintage bedding

Our children love tucking little teddies and dolls up into their own beds. And even the youngest one thinks that they are not the first to go to sleep when teddy has already been safely snuggled into bed before them. These little bedding sets are modelled on the sorts of sheets and blankets that were used before duvets, so you can add as many layers as you like.

There are often vintage cots to be found on internet auction sites, but don't be put off if you cannot find one; doll's prams, new cots or even a big shoe box covered in paper seem to please just as well.

Some cots may be painted with old lead paint, so choose carefully when purchasing vintage items. This paint is toxic if ingested, either by chewing something painted with it or by breathing in the dust created if it is sanded. Advice varies, but as long as the original paint is in good condition, a couple of coats of gloss or acrylic paint over the top of any old paint is probably the best way forwards. If you need to sand the original paint, then look on the internet for appropriate instructions.

BLANKET

1. Measure the base of the cot that you want to make bedding for and make a paper template.

2. Cut the blanket fabric to size using the template – use any existing satin trim or stitching as the top hem, if possible. Blanket stitch (see page 21) all the way around cut edges or add ribbon trim, if you like.

SHEETS AND PILLOWS

1. To make a sheet cut fabric twice the size of the template you made in step 1, for the blanket (see above) and turn under a double hem all the way around. Press it flat and sew all around with a sewing machine set to a small straight stitch. (You could also make a sheet from an old tray cloth or hem a piece of embroidered tablecloth that is no longer used.)

2. To make two pillows cut another fabric piece the size of the template, fold it in quarters and cut along the folds to make the backs and fronts of two pillows. With right sides facing, sew each pair of rectangles together nearly all the way around. Turn them right sides out, fill them with polyester stuffing, then hand-sew up the openings.

EIDERDOWN

1. Cut out two rectangles of pretty print fabric using the guide. With right sides facing and taking a narrow seam allowance, sew the rectangles together on the sewing machine, leaving an opening of about 15cm at the bottom end. Turn the eiderdown right sides out.

2. Cut a rectangle of wadding, or a couple of layers of woollen blanket, to the right size to fit inside the eiderdown and then pop the wadding inside the cover and push it out right to the corners and edges. Hand-sew or use the sewing machine to close the opening along the bottom end. Finish off the eiderdown by machine-sewing neat little lines in a traditional quilt pattern right through the layers of wadding and fabric. You can add little trims, frills and initials, too, if you like.

MATTRESS

If you need a mattress for the bed, use the template used for the blanket (see left) to cut two rectangles from a thicker canvas or ticking fabric. Make up a mattress in just the same way as the eiderdown, but add more layers of wadding to make it a bit thicker. Instead of sewing the quilt pattern, simply hand-sew through all the layers in a couple of places to hold the filling in place.

Press all the bedding neatly, fold it up into a little stack and tie it together with a ribbon.

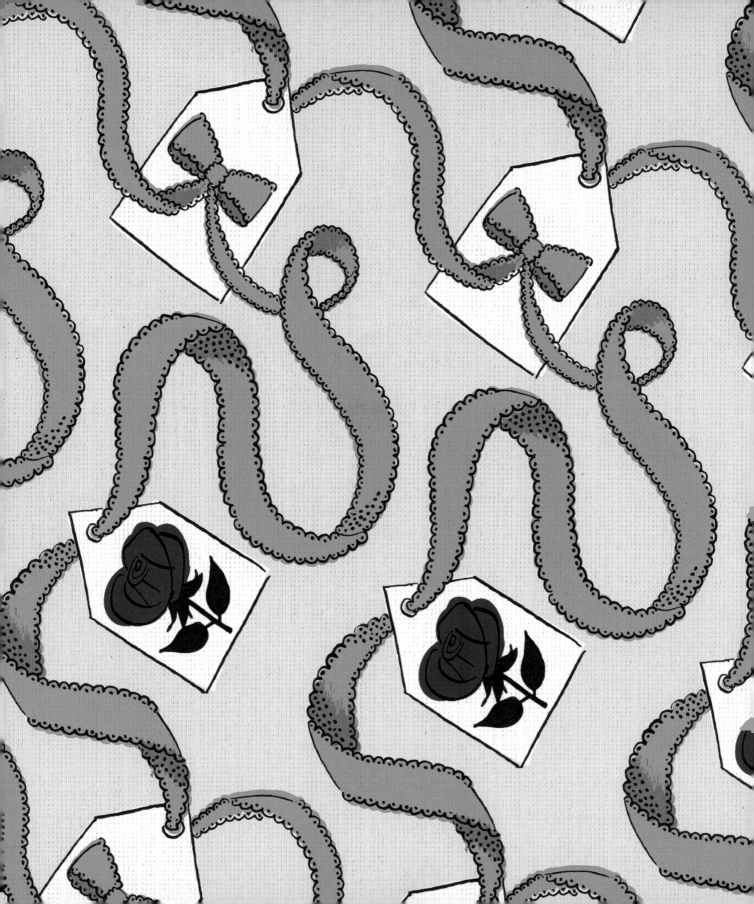

CARDS
AND
PACKAGING

button & silhouette cards

SIMPLE SILHOUETTE CARDS

There are some simple silhouettes that you can make from vintage materials to make great gift cards. Strong shapes that are easily recognisable seem to work best. Use a blank plain card or carefully cut and fold your own. Buy envelopes or make them as on page 156. Decide on the style of image you want on the card: hearts, butterflies, crosses, wedding bells or even straightforward squares of interestingly patterned wallpaper, maps or fabric look really effective, and numbers and initials make your cards personal too.

1. Draw the design in pencil on the back of whatever material you choose, remembering to reverse letters and numbers where required. If you need some extra help, try finding an image online or in the papers that you can follow the outline of or trace; you can try drawing around biscuit cutters, as there is one of those for nearly every occasion.

2. Using sharp scissors or a craft knife, carefully cut around the pencil line.

3. Apply a thin layer of PVA glue to the back of the motif and stick it firmly in place on the front of the card. Allow to dry completely.

BUTTON CARDS

I have always loved the combination of sewing and paper, so this might be why I like making these button cards.

1. Collect some pretty buttons that go well together and suit your design. Arrange them in the pattern or motif as they will appear on the front of the card. Once again, initials and numbers work well, as do easily recognisable shapes such as Christmas trees and flowers. You can draw onto the card, to add detail.

3. Once decided on your design, sew the buttons onto the card in just the way that you would if you were using fabric. Fasten off the thread by tying a knot on the back of the card. When you are finished, stick a single piece of card onto the inside to cover up the back of the stitching or line the whole card with wallpaper.

wallpaper envelopes

Wallpapers, particularly of the bold, printed variety, are so useful to have. If you are lucky enough to find whole rolls of the stuff that you don't want to use on your walls, then you probably won't mind using some to make envelopes. For the neatest results, track down some pre-folded and cut cards from a craft supplier.

1. Carefully pull apart the seams of the envelope and flatten it out to create a template. Draw around the outline onto the back of the wallpaper, then cut out the shape.

2. Fold it along the same lines as the template back into an envelope and use thin strips of double-sided tape to stick it together. Add more double-sided tape where you normally find the gummed section, leaving the top paper layer of the tape in place until you are ready to stick down the flap.

gift tags

All parcels need to be properly labelled. So pop your gift on the present table with a lovely tag attached.

Old-fashioned luggage labels can come in all sorts of colours and sizes. Buy some of these, or make your own from stiff card and embellish them on one side with snippets of wallpaper, ribbon, lace trims and buttons. Or decorate them like mini versions of the cards on pages 154-5. Make a place for the ribbon in one end with a hole punch and thread through a little length of trimming to secure your tag to the present.

YOU WILL NEED:

wallpaper | brown paper and string | hand-printed wrapping paper | fabric bags (see page 105) | covered boxes | lined baskets (see page 91) | ribbons | corsages (see pages 74-6) | handmade tags (see page 159)

gift wrapping

If you have spent hours making and searching for vintage gifts, you will want to make them look beautiful when they are wrapped up.

If you are after a retro feeling on the outside of the wrapping as well as on the inside, anything from vintage wallpaper to glazed chintz can be used for wrapping. Collect and cover little boxes and keep your eyes open for old packaging too. Lined wicker baskets or picnic hampers can all be filled with treasures as well.

Gather together lengths of ribbon, pretty twine, bias binding, pieces of lace and vintage trimmings and use them to tie your securely wrapped presents. Add little brooches, sparkly buckles, corsages and gift tags to really gild the lily.

templates

Over the next few pages are a small selection of outlines that you might find useful.

Some projects that mention templates in the book are more straightforward, but here are tried-and-tested patterns for the gingerbread man and the lavender bunny that will create your own gorgeous versions of the ones seen on pages 86, 110 and 113. Plus there are a few helpful, hearts, shields and hexagons for other projects.

Use tracing paper to copy the outlines, or scan or photocopy the templates before cutting out your copies. Place or pin the paper onto your material and use tailor's chalk to mark the sewing line around the edges. These patterns are all symmetrical, but for projects elsewhere in the book like the gloves and Christmas stocking, where you have a 'good' side to the material, check that everything is the right way round before you cut. Keep your templates for future use too.

gifts for occasions

MOTHER'S DAY

Mother's Day Sewing Basket
with Pin Cushions &
Needle Books

Fabric-covered Diaries
& Notebooks

Lavender Cushions & Hanger

FATHER'S DAY

Cufflinks

Homemade Jams & Jellies

VALENTINE'S DAY

Picnic Hamper

Beaded Door Hanger

Corsages

EASTER

Easter Egg Cups

HOUSEWARMING

Tea Cosy and Teapot

Covered Hangers & Shoe Trees

Tapestry Cushions

Laundry Bags

Layered Cake Stands

Pretty Lamp

Patchwork Noticeboard

Plate Hangers

Teacup Candles

Decanterlabras

BABY SHOWER

Baby Blankets

Lavender Bunnies

Hanging Mobiles

BIRTHDAYS

Hat, Scarf & Mittens

Easy Peasy Lace Trim Choker

Dog & Cat Cushions

Hot Water Bottle Covers

Little Covered Suitcase

Fabric Pictures

CHILDREN'S BIRTHDAYS

Baker's Apron &
Biscuit Mixture

Little Girl's Easy Skirt

Re-rigged Old Boats

Doll's Vintage Bedding

Pencil Rolls

Beads & Baubles Kits

Coat of Arms

HOUSE GUEST

Apothecary Bottles
& Decanter Shampoos

Guest Soaps

Planters for Christmas & Spring

Gifts for a Weekend Away

CHRISTMAS

Christmas Stockings

Advent Calendar

Christmas Decorations

Christmas Wreaths

suppliers

BORN IN THE CHAPEL SARAH MOORE

Very vintage finds, blog and inspirational ideas for making more homemade gifts with vintage style.

www.borninthechapel.co.uk

IACF INTERNATIONAL ANTIQUES AND COLLECTORS FAIRS

Nationwide antiques fairs on a massive scale.

www.iacf.co.uk

Check online for the next and nearest fair to you.

CARBOOTJUNCTION. COM

Straightforward website listing over 2000 car boot sales.

www.carbootjunction.com

LINDA CLIFT ANTIQUE TEXTILES

Carries a wide range of fabrics, trims and buttons. Stock includes English, American and French quilts; French linens, tickings and fabrics; blankets, handmade throws, paisley shawls and vintage clothes and accessories.

www.antiquequiltsandtextiles.co.uk
textile@lindaclift.co.uk

LIZ VAN HASSELT

Antique and Vintage Textiles, Costume & Accessories, 1900 - 1980. Blog giving details of lots of vintage textiles fairs where Liz sells her treasures.

www.thewasherwoman. blogspot.com
JLTG40@aol.com

STABLE ANTIQUES

Perfect vintage hunting ground for affordable antiques, quirky collectables and kitchenalia.

46 West Street, Storrington West Sussex, RH20 4EE UK

www.stableantiques.co.uk

01903 740 555

VINTAGE LIFESTYLE

www.vintagelifestyle.co.uk

01722 417 907

Great online store that sells faded floral textiles, worn painted furniture and all things vintage.

DONNA FLOWER

Online textiles fair that stocks vintage fabrics and homewares from the turn of the last century

www.donnaflower.com

0845 4735095

VINTAGE HOME

Original, authentic and iconic homewares all on display on a bright and beautiful website.

www.vintage-home.co.uk

01432 830 236

WWW.EBAY.CO.UK

The UK's largest online auction site for everything new, used and lots of vintage items.

HOME AND COLONIAL

134 High Street, Berkhamsted, Hertfordshire, HP4 3AT

www.homeandcolonial.co.uk

01442 877 007

Great mix of interiors and antiques, with more than a few vintage items in between.

index